,50

JESUS GIRLS

EXPERIENCES *in* EVANGELICALISM

edited by CHRISTOPHER J. KELLER *and* ANDREW DAVID

The Experiences in Evangelicalism series offers forays into the evangelical experience, rethinking and reimagining key questions, practices, and tenets of faith, as they have been framed in the evangelical tradition. Through theological reflection, critical analysis, and personal narrative, the series seeks to craft a more authentic and engaging evangelical spirituality. This series is a working partnership between *The Other Journal* at Mars Hill Graduate School and Cascade Books.

JESUS GIRLS

True Tales of Growing Up
Female and Evangelical

EDITED BY

Hannah Faith Notess

CASCADE *Books* · Eugene, Oregon

JESUS GIRLS
True Tales of Growing Up Female and Evangelical

Experiences in Evangelicalism 1

Cascade Books
A Division of Wipf and Stock Publishers
199 W. 8th Ave., Suite 3
Eugene, OR 97401

www.wipfandstock.com

ISBN 13: 978-1-60608-541-7

All scripture quotations, unless otherwise indicated, are from *New Revised Standard Version Bible*, copyright © 1989, Division of Christian Education of the National Council of the Churches of Christ in the United States of America. Used by permission. All rights reserved.

Cataloging-in-Publication data:

Jesus girls : true tales of growing up female and evangelical / edited by Hannah Faith Notess.

xiv + 224 p. ; 23 cm.

Experiences in Evangelicalism 1

ISBN 13: 978-1-60608-541-7

1. Women—Religious aspects—Christianity. 2. Feminism—Religious aspects—Christianity. 3. Evangelicalism. 4. Women in Christianity. I. Title. II. Series.

BT704. J51 2009

Manufactured in the U.S.A.

Contents

A WOMAN WHO FEARS THE LORD—GENDER AND SEX

THE VOICE OF ONE CRYING IN THE WILDERNESS—
STORY AND IDENTITY

Acknowledgments

Grateful acknowledgment is given to the editors of the periodicals in which several of these essays first appeared:

"Dead End" by Jessica Belt first appeared in *Relief* in 2009.

"Going Way against the Flow" by Anne Dayton first appeared in *Geez* in 2009.

"Why Isn't God like Eric Clapton?" by Andrea Palpant Dilley first appeared in *Rock and Sling* in 2008.

"Inventing a Testimony" by Melanie Springer Mock first appeared in *Ruminate* in 2007 as "The Perils of Testimony."

"Swimming Lessons" by Victoria Moon first appeared in *Louisville Review* in 2005.

"Keep the Feast" by Nicole Sheets first appeared in *Pilgrimage* in 2006.

"Heal Me" by Stephanie Tombari first appeared in *Geez* in 2006.

"Seamless" by Jessie van Eerden first appeared in *The Other Journal* in 2009.

"Who Is My Mother, Who Are My Brothers?" by Sara Zarr first appeared in *Image* in 2009.

Appreciation is also expressed to Zondervan for granting permission to reprint "Spark" by Shauna Niequist, which first appeared as the second chapter in *Cold Tangerines: Celebrating the Extraordinary Nature of Everyday Life* (Zondervan, 2007).

Thanks to the many people whose help and support made this book possible. Without the assistance, enthusiasm, and careful editorial attention of Chris Keller, Andrew David, Chris Spinks, and the other staff of *The Other Journal* at Mars Hill Graduate School and Cascade Books, the book might never have seen print.

Many people provided assistance in discovering writers, feedback on the manuscript, and other invaluable forms of guidance, including Scott Russell Sanders, Paul Willis, Debra Rienstra, Doug Frank, Amanda Sparkman, Ahna Phillips, Shannon Hill, Greg Wolfe, and Donna Freitas, among others.

I am very grateful to the MFA in Creative Writing Program at Indiana University and the Milton Center at *Image Journal* and Seattle Pacific University for providing me time and space to put this book together.

Many thanks are also due to the contributors for being so patient, so dedicated to their writing, and so enthusiastic about the project. It has been a pleasure to work with all of them!

Thanks to my family for loving and encouraging me no matter what, and thanks to Jonathan Hiskes, my wonderful husband, who supported me during the entire process.

—HFN

Introduction
Un-Testimonies

by Hannah Faith Notess

Growing up in evangelical churches meant I was trained to tell the story of my life. That story was called a testimony, for which the rough formula was "I once was lost but now am found, was blind but now I see." John Newton, the man who penned that hymn, had a spectacular testimony himself. He had been captain of a slave ship, a profiteer of torture and atrocity, and he had renounced his evil deeds after, as we put it, he accepted Jesus into his heart. The basic narrative of evangelical experience has survived virtually unchanged in this form for several centuries, longer if you count the famous conversion stories of Saints Paul and Augustine. When I was growing up, the best testimonies came from ex-angry young men, ex-drug addicts, ex-fornicators, et cetera. The more spectacularly wicked you had been, the better Jesus looked for having saved you.

As a kid, I was pretty sure I hadn't been wicked enough to have a real testimony. But all Christians have a testimony, a well-meaning Sunday school teacher once told me. The implication, of course, was that if you didn't have a testimony, you weren't a Christian.

But, as it happened, I really *didn't* have a testimony. I had been attending church since I was an embryo, and I had been loving God and trying, more or less, to be good the entire time. When, at age five, I took the all-important step of asking Jesus into my heart, nothing in particular seemed to happen. I tried asking a few more times, then gave up, figuring he *must* be in my heart by now. I was pretty sure, if you asked, he wouldn't say "no." But there was no change in my life—not even the warm feeling inside that I had been so sure would come.

When I got asked to share my testimony in Sunday school, or later on, as a summer camp counselor, I said I had been bad before asking Jesus into my heart. I had embellished my picture-books with crayon; I had thrown toys at my brother; I had run with scissors. Or, in some unspecified way, I had "realized I was a sinner." But I was lying. I hadn't realized I was a sinner, because back then I'd barely had any time to sin. Before my attempts to invite Jesus into my heart, I was actually less of a sinner than after the fact, having had less time to sin. The truth was I had always tried to love God, and for all my love and God's love, I was really no better or worse than I'd been before.

So what can I call the story of my spiritual life, if not a testimony? Well . . . how about an un-testimony? An un-testimony is not a story of reverse conversion. Dazzled-by-the-light Christian conversion stories aren't much different from dazzled-by-science atheistic conversion stories. It's just that in one, the formula is "wasn't life awful, and I'm so glad Jesus saved me," and in the other, the formula is "wasn't life awful, and I'm so glad I escaped those religious freaks." No, an un-testimony is an unruly story, a story that refuses to conform to a simple before-and-after pattern. An un-testimony is the story of a journey that is not necessarily linear, may not have a tidy resolution, and may not lead to an earth-shattering change in our beliefs.

I put this book together out of the conviction that those of us with un-testimonies still have stories to tell. In fact, I'd argue that the testimony is an especially awkward form for those of us raised in the evangelical church. I prayed the sinner's prayer at age five. But I just can't be convinced that moment was the climax in the narrative of my spiritual life. Many of the writers in this book find themselves wrestling with doubt and faith for years, still living with questions of belief to which there are no pat answers.

Another problem with conversion narratives is that the cast of characters is so small and predictable. The two lead roles are always played by the sinner and God, with a few godly individuals, like Saint Augustine's mother Monica, playing bit parts to nudge the sinner along the path. But in real life, nobody encounters God in a vacuum. Even churches that emphasize a "Jesus and me" theology still function as communities. In church, people laugh, cry, gossip, argue about theology, fall in love, and do a whole host of other ordinary activities, right alongside their praying and worshipping, if not mixed up with it. To tell the story of growing up evangelical is to tell about the church, about the people around us—whether they lived up to our expectations or not.

Defining evangelicalism is problematic, of course. In this book, it's defined loosely. The communities in which these writers were raised—Sara Zarr's hippie, Jesus-freak church, Carla-Elaine Johnson's African Methodist Episcopal and Missionary Baptist roots, or Kirsten Cruzen's missionary-kid boarding school—span a wide range of beliefs and practices. All of these writers' experiences fit within some form of North American Protestantism that emphasizes the Bible, conversion, saving souls, and one or another of the doctrinal distinctives of evangelicalism. Additionally, some of these writers initially approached evangelicalism as outsiders: Audrey Molina and Kimberly B. George came to evangelicalism as teenagers at youth group rather than as children. Stephanie Tombari stepped outside her United Church of Canada upbringing to attend a healing service at Toronto Airport Christian Fellowship, a Pentecostal church. Still, I am painfully aware of the limits of this book. There are many groups of people within North American evangelicalism whose voices are not included and whose experiences are not described in this collection.

I limited this collection to stories by women writers for a few reasons. First, among evangelical speakers and writers, there are far more men than women. Even in evangelical circles that approve of women's leadership, it seems, too often women are only called upon to speak on "women's issues." Some of the writers in this collection, like Heather Baker Utley and Shari MacDonald Strong, reflect on experiences that relate specifically to being a woman in the evangelical church; others, like Anastasia McAteer and Andrea Saylor, write on topics unrelated to gender.

The second reason for limiting this collection to women writers is that testimony and spiritual autobiography have been historically significant ways for women to speak up in evangelical circles. Even in churches where Paul's injunction that "women should be silent in the churches" has been taken very seriously, if not literally, the testimony has been one of the most common ways a woman's voice can be heard in the church, one of the most common ways women have been able to share their spiritual insight with other Christians.

Those of us with un-testimonies have epiphanies, too, but they don't necessarily involve being blinded by the light on the road to Damascus. Some of us find our Christian faith growing stronger as the years pass, while others of us find ourselves drifting away from the churches in which we were raised. We may find spiritual sustenance in unlikely places, like the community swimming pool or a Muslim pilgrimage site. At the same time, we may find ourselves unmoved when we're supposed to be carried away—by praise choruses or prayer meetings. But these moments aren't edited out of the story. Instead, they're part of the story.

My hope is that these stories will provide a new window into the evangelical experience, while challenging people of faith to reconsider how they tell their own stories, whether their lives fit a before-and-after pattern, or whether their lives are an unfolding narrative whose arc is only beginning to take shape.

Where Two
or Three
Are Gathered

COMMUNITY

1

Who Is My
Mother,
Who Are My
Brothers?

by Sara Zarr

On the day of my baptism, my father stood at the back of the church—hung-over, or quite possibly drunk even at that early hour—and shouted, "Hooray for Sara!" as I came up out of the water. I was eight years old.

That's how my mother remembers it. My memories are less dramatic: the heavy white robe I wore that was more like a thick doctor's coat than anything resembling the drapey garb of the flannelgraph versions of Jesus and his disciples I knew from Sunday school; stepping down into the chlorinated blue water of the baptismal; holding onto the solid forearm of my pastor as I followed his instructions—bend your knees, lean back, close your eyes, try to relax.

I did it because I'd seen other people at church do it. I did it for my mom, for my Sunday school teacher, and also because I truly believed, at eight, that I was ready to make a public declaration of my faith. That's how I understood baptism: you believed in Jesus and then you proved it. I'm sure my father saw it as something even simpler—his youngest daughter mimicking her mother. What he didn't realize—what even I would only come to grasp years later—was that he was witnessing a transfer of allegiance. When I came up out of the water, soaked and relieved to have not gotten any water up my nose, I was a member of a different family, the daughter of a different father.

• • •

There's a scene in the Gospel of Matthew. Jesus is talking to a crowd. The topics are difficult and complex—the Sabbath, the devil, signs, miracles. Out of the blue, someone tells Jesus that his mother and brothers are standing outside waiting to talk to him. Jesus replies, "Who is my mother, and who are my brothers?" He points to the disciples and says, "Here are my mother and my brothers! For whoever does the will of my Father in heaven is my brother and sister and mother." In Luke's telling, Jesus pulls no punches. "Whoever comes to me and does not hate father and mother, wife and children, brothers and sisters, yes, and even life itself, cannot be my disciple."

In either version, the point is made. When you follow Jesus everything changes, including and perhaps especially the strongest, most natural ties a creature can have.

This notion of the church, fellow believers, as my family was ingrained early. No small part of that was a function of time and place. I grew up in San Francisco in the seventies, the cradle of the Jesus Movement. The Bay Area was full of orphaned flower children— hippies disillusioned by the drug and free-love scene that had failed them, but still seeking the ideals of community that the sixties had promised. Some of these seekers found faith in Jesus and infused it with their nonconformist approach to living, and soon Christian coffee houses, street evangelism, folk-inspired worship songs, and the rejection of confining church tradition all added up to a bona fide social phenomenon: the California Jesus Freak. And I was one of them, or at least, among them.

Our little Bible church was a mix of these born-again hippies, neighborhood natives, a few church ladies, and a handful of families that, like mine, had landed in San Francisco from other parts of the country. We had moved there in 1972, taking up residence in a roomy one-bedroom flat that a family like ours would never be able to afford today. It was my parents' last stop on a journey that had started in North Carolina and Pennsylvania and taken them through Ohio and Indiana, a road littered with the remains of my father's career and relationships all but ruined by his drinking. San Francisco was as far west as a pioneering spirit could go—literally and philosophically. Somewhere on that journey my mother became a born-again Christian; my father did not. He didn't have any real objections, though, and my mother took us to and raised us in this neighborhood church.

Two prominent features on the landscape of seventies Christianity were the Second Chapter of Acts and the second chapter of Acts: the former, three siblings who made up one of the first contemporary Christian music groups and inspired the creation of many, many who would come after; the latter, part of the biblical chronicle of the early church that includes a description of believers selling their possessions and sharing all they had, meeting in one another's homes and breaking bread with "glad and generous hearts." Jesus Movement churches took this passage to heart, and most of our family bonding happened in the homes of members during the week. We'd crowd into each other's apartments for food, singing, prayer, and "sharing"—the distinctly post-sixties way of talking about God's work in our lives, how he spoke to us through the Bible and fellow believers, and the challenges of living our faith daily.

When my mom became the church secretary, I spent hour upon hour in the building after school, exploring all the little corners and closets, crawling on my belly under pews, stealing up to the balcony for a nap or to look again at the maroon choir robes that I'd never seen used and that had a smell I can only describe as pigeony. Though I liked the sense of privilege, the hours I spent there were also lonely and symptomatic of my family's problems. My father, deep into his drinking, couldn't be counted on to take care of me, or to provide for the family, so Mom had to work and the church was the only safe place for me to go after school. It was free of the alcohol-related anxieties that went with being home, but it wasn't home. The building was a sanctuary for me, but also a place of exile, because I wouldn't have been there if our family's situation hadn't been quite so desperate. Under different circumstances and if our blood relatives weren't so far away, maybe we wouldn't have run so quickly and completely into the embrace of spiritual family. Maybe it wasn't so much about running toward something, into sanctuary, but away from something, into a comforting sort of exile that was, at the time, our only option.

Whatever it was—sanctuary, exile, or a little of both—it was genuine and the center of our lives.

Our little slice of Acts 2, the home fellowship evenings, did not exclude children. My sister and I sat cross-legged on a shag carpet or reclined against beanbag chairs many an evening and listened to adult stories of drug abuse, sexual debauchery, broken families, and failed attempts at right living. Everyone had testimony—a story about how hopeless, empty, and appalling their lives were before they found God, or God found them, and lifted them out of their sin.

The sharing and the testimonies and the prayers were my family stories. They asked and answered questions about who I was and where I'd come from and what my life would be about. What I heard, over and over, was this: Jesus lives. Jesus saves. Jesus loves, and loves me. I heard that even the most depraved, screwed-up lives were not beyond his saving grace and love. No one could go so far over the edge that they wouldn't be welcomed, like the prodigal son, back into the father's household. This knowledge, those testimonies, created one of the fundamental tensions of my childhood. Yes, my father was a sinner with a drinking problem, but at any moment he could have an experience like those I heard about in the home groups—a shock of recognition followed by surrender and the sinner's prayer—and he'd finally be part of our family, too. The possibility of his salvation, remote as it felt, hovered over every story and testimony that I heard. *Maybe next time*, I would think, *it will be him.*

• • •

One shadow lurked over and beneath all of the bonding and sharing and pot-lucking: the end times.

An obsession with end times theology was a hallmark of the seventies Jesus Movement. Hal Lindsey's 1970 book *The Late, Great Planet Earth* was a monster bestseller of the decade—*The Purpose-Driven Life* of its day, only with a profoundly disturbing message.

Lindsey explored biblical prophesies about the end of the world and drew the conclusion that the apocalypse was mere moments away. The world was in for a good seven years of tribulation, complete with plagues, wars, and famines—unless you were a believer, in which case you'd be raptured. One second you'd be brushing your teeth, the next your pajamas would be a puddle on the floor, your unsaved friends and family looking on, dumbfounded. We heard constantly in sermons, small groups, and conversation about the rapture, the Antichrist, the mark of the Beast, the tribulation, the millennium, the second coming of Jesus.

I couldn't imagine a future for myself, as I doubted I'd inhabit the planet through the week, never mind past eighteen. The horsemen and trumpets and Christ himself would be glorious, *if* I could remain faithful—*if*, in my own Peter-esque moments, I was strong enough to claim Christ and not deny him. When all my unbelieving friends were lining up to receive the mark of the Beast, would I have the courage to say no? Would I be willing to face torture, imprisonment, or even death for the sake of my Savior? Knowing intimately my fundamental weaknesses as a human, I was pretty sure I'd be one of the sad, weak people who buckled early in the tribulation. Before age ten I'd already accumulated a lengthy roster of sin: stealing candy from the corner store, lying to my mom about how much TV I watched, calling the telephone operator and swearing at her, gossiping at school, reading from the copy of *Penthouse Stories* circulating at school. If I couldn't resist a candy bar, how would I withstand the genuine trials that were sure to come?

Our fear and trembling about Christ's return and the accompanying separation of wheat and chaff had another implication: each person's salvation was subject to eventual authentication. Even someone who *appeared* to be "in the family" might have a heart of darkness that would leave them behind while you were caught up in the clouds. After all, it says right in the Bible that "Not everyone who says to me, 'Lord! Lord!' will enter the kingdom of heaven, but only the one who does the will of my Father in heaven." The sense of impending world destruction created a heightened desire to be absolutely sure that you and the people in your spiritual family were really headed for the mansion in the sky and not the Other Place.

More than once, I heard about various church members who were "backsliding," a term that seemed to mean anything from relapsing into drug use to missing a few Sundays in a row.

My angst over backsliders (including, possibly, me) was not helped by the Jack Chick tracts that surfaced everywhere during that time. I was mesmerized and horrified by the most ubiquitous of them: *This Was Your Life*. In it, a man is visited by the grim reaper, then taken by an angel to his appointment with judgment, where he watches as though on a movie screen every sinful moment of his life. In the end, even though people thought he was a good person, and he went to church on Sundays, he is tossed into the lake of fire. This punishment seems to be the direct result of enjoying a cocktail, telling a dirty joke as a teenager, and wondering who was winning a football game instead of paying attention to a sermon in church. The last few pages of the tract depicted an alternate life for this man, in which he prays to receive Christ, visits the elderly, reads the Bible to children, and witnesses to the unsaved. The back included a prayer one could recite and thereby attain salvation. I said the prayer every time I saw it, just in case.

Ironically, those of us in that movement really thought we got it, thought that we more than anyone understood the gospel and all of its implications. We talked about grace and about other churches and their "legalism." Looking back it seemed what grace meant to us was being able to wear jeans to church and play the guitar. We still didn't really get it. At least I didn't. The more information I absorbed from various quarters, the more I believed it didn't take all that much for a person to move from being right in the center of the family to being more like a distant cousin, then a black sheep, and eventually not in the family photo at all. The one comfort was that as far as I knew, those who left did so by choice. The church's open door worked both ways—anyone seeking Jesus could come in, and anyone who decided they needed to leave was free to do just that.

This proved to be the case with my biological family, too. Shortly after the eighties began, my father left us for good, returning to Pennsylvania without a California testimony.

• • •

The final nail in the coffin of idealized seventies Christianity, for me, came in the summer of 1982. While visiting my father and grandmother in Pennsylvania, I hid in my father's childhood bedroom while they fought, and watched TV. A news report came on: Christian singer Keith Green—who I idolized, and had seen in concert—two of his children, and nine other people had died in a small-plane crash while Green was showing off his Last Days Ministries property.

It didn't seem possible. My parents were divorced, the Cold War was coming to a frightening crescendo, Keith Green was dead, and, Hal Lindsey notwithstanding, Jesus hadn't come back yet. Where did that leave us?

In the suburbs, eventually, where we moved when my mother remarried. We still attended and participated in my childhood church but it was different. With people moving out of the city and having kids and real jobs and real money and real mid-life crises, home gatherings were no longer so convenient. There was a sense that we'd given Acts 2 our best, naïve shot, and it was time to move on. Not that those ideals were completely discarded—I think members of that church still believed there was no point just showing up Sunday mornings if you weren't going to share your life with anyone. Efforts were made. It was just that other things were now allowed to get in the way. After all, if we weren't actually as close to the end times as we'd thought, there was no longer any real *rush*.

And, as it turned out, you could fight with your church family as readily as with your biological family. It was frighteningly easy, in fact, to lose touch with anyone you wanted to lose touch with, or anyone who wanted to lose touch with you. Disagreements about minor or major doctrinal differences, arguments over whether or not to invest in new chairs or hymnals, the content of Sunday school curriculum, plain boredom . . . anything could be an excuse to leave if that's what you wanted.

My disillusionment was complete when the pastor I'd grown up with left in a church split. I don't remember the specifics of the issue, just that discussions were heated, meetings endless, emotions high. Members were left wounded and questioning whether anything we'd experienced during the good old days was as authentic and meaningful as we'd believed while it was all happening. Some wanted to prolong and duplicate past experiences; others wanted to get out and start fresh somewhere else. Those of us who stayed became more protective of ourselves and our stories. Why couldn't we "go home again," even though we'd never left, even though a spiritual family was supposed to be a reflection of something different, better, eternal, and redeemed?

As an adult, after having been a member of three or four different churches and having seen more politics, splits, and failures, I've begun to understand the fly in the church-family ointment. I grew up loving and believing in the church as much as I believed in God, maybe more. Jesus had become synonymous with churches' names, pastors, worship styles, and congregants. My experience of a particular expression of Christianity had come to replace faith.

In the scene in Matthew where Jesus tells the crowd who his real family is, maybe we had focused on the wrong part of the story. We grasped at the part about being brothers and sisters because that's what we understood, and it sounded appealing and right. Especially in the seventies, it fit in with the ideals of peace, love, and understanding. Doing the will of the Father was the part we perhaps paid less attention to. And maybe Luke's harsh, hard-to-read version is more helpful in the end: "hating" anything, anyone, that ends up coming before or between following Jesus, is the only way to avoid the problems that come with the almost idolatrous worship of "the community."

Though the creation of a utopian society based on two verses in the book of Acts is probably just another way to deny that we need grace every second in order to be at all Christlike, I still tend to gravitate toward churches that attempt to act like families. It would be easier, honestly, *not* to. Because once you find your congregation and commit and make this public claim of family, and moreover once you start living like you believe what it says in the Bible about unity and the body of Christ, you open your life in every way to exactly the kind of pain and grief and frustration and inconvenience that we all spend so much time trying to avoid. Life is difficult enough without taking on the problems of a dozen or thirty or fifty or two hundred people who aren't even your relatives, and being part of a church family brings at least as many problems as it soothes. Why would I seek that, rather than simply slipping into a different church each Sunday, no one knowing my name or my life story? Maybe because it's what I know, or maybe something mystical did happen in my baptism, joining me to this family that reaches across space and time. And given the model of adoption laid out in John 1, I'm pretty sure that this is the kind of family that isn't about me choosing it, but it choosing me.

My father died at Thanksgiving, 2005, alone, still alienated from family—biological or otherwise. As far as I know, he never had the conversion experience we'd hoped and prayed for, and the instructions he left with the funeral home were brief: cremation, and no memorial or funeral or religious services of any kind were to be held. My allegiance lying elsewhere, the first person I contacted was my pastor, asking him to help arrange a brief and simple service to observe my father's passing. Within hours, members of my church—a Presbyterian church in Salt Lake City, years and miles and cultures away from the Bible church of my childhood—turned up with flowers, urns of coffee, cookies. Our house filled with people who never even met my dad but were connected to him and his story through me, familial ties extending in ways that can't be charted on a family tree. We all walked the several blocks from our house to a nearby cemetery, where we picked a spot on a hill to pray and read a Psalm.

My sister and I had visited my father in the hospital the night before he died, and though at the time we had no idea that was what we were doing, we were able to make some sort of peace. That's not easy when your father will barely look you in the eye, speak a sentence that indicates any interest in your life, or admit to profound failures. The promise of family and adoption inherent in baptism—the promise of belonging to Jesus—allowed us a kind of compassion for our dad we most certainly would not have been able to muster had we been relying on him to head our family. It's that contrast, between the way things are when we're on our own and the way they can be when we're God's, that keeps me looking to my church to be my family. Even in its most dysfunctional moments, a Christ-centered church family seems infinitely more right than a flailing biological one. With every Sunday service, potluck, home group, or hillside memorial, there's a momentary glimpse of a dim reflection of the glory of true home, where hating your mother and father might actually make sense, given how short they, and we, fall. Why would a bunch of Christians stand in a cemetery remembering the life of a man who disdained their faith, a man who didn't even want to be mourned? I think it was—and in all our attempts at family-making, is—our way of saying: this is how it could be, this is how it should be, this is how it will be when Christ finally does return, and all our families are redeemed.

2

Open the
Doors
and See All the
People

by Paula Carter

When I was fourteen, our church, the Evangelical Free Church of Geneseo, split. About half of our church members left and went off to form their own church, and when that didn't work out, they went to other established churches. One Sunday they were there, and then, like the rapture, they were gone. I imagined these people wandering away from our church in a crowd. I could see them slowly traversing the soggy ground of the cornfield to the west of our small church, a field that also abutted the high school a mile away, which is where the group met for a few months, setting up in the gymnasium. When I imagine the split, I imagine the Harpels and the Darbys and the Junises all walking away with angry faces, raising their fists in the air like a mob.

I still don't know exactly why our church split. The split happened in the summer, the summer before my first year of high school. My impressions of it are vague, like my made-up mob. I have to ask my mother to fill in the details and remind me of the chronology.

What I do remember about the summer our church split is my junior high Sunday school class. Our teacher was a big man, funny and childish. He was young, probably in his mid-thirties, but that seemed ancient to those of us in his class who were still trying to

13

guess what high school would be like. He liked to goof around, joking with us and being silly, trying to get us to open up about our teenaged lives. The classroom was in the basement of the church, damp and chilly with painted cement brick walls and a cement floor covered by pieces of fraying gold carpet. I was always cold in the basement, wearing a skirt and thin hose, which I thought made me look more grown up.

One of the first things we would do is pray. Our teacher would take prayer requests. I always hated prayer requests. I felt obligated to have a request, like I was somehow not trusting God with my problems if I didn't. But at the same time, I felt annoyed with the other requests, which always seemed trivial and gossipy to me: "Pray for my brother as he drives back to college this afternoon." "Pray for my aunt's broken leg." "Pray for a friend of mine, whose name I'd rather not say, who is starting to get involved in some bad things." Everyone in the class knew each other well. We all went to the same school, knew each other's friends, and for the most part, had been in Sunday school classes together since we were small children. A prayer request about a "friend" started everyone guessing. It also allowed the person making the request to sit up straight and give knowing nods, to be the one with the inside scoop, the one who was in church and not doing those bad things. We all understood that we must silently disapprove of this friend—who was either not a Christian or had strayed.

After taking the requests, our teacher would dole them out. We all took one. Then we would pray, our teacher wrapping it up with an attempt to invoke the Spirit. Most of my Sunday school teachers were great at this: "I just want to praise God that I've been given this opportunity to be with these young people today. Guide our time together . . ." But my junior high teacher lacked inspiration. Sometimes he asked someone else to finish for him, or he ended safely by praising the beautiful day.

He was a new Christian, and to be honest, I'm not sure how he came to teach the junior high Sunday school class. He seemed far more bewildered by the Bible than we were. Often we would sit around discussing some vaguely spiritual topic, which might turn into a discussion about movies or teachers or friends. But at times he would try to put together serious lessons. For these lessons, it was obvious he had worked hard and had a specific goal in mind, leading us toward it by force, if he had to.

Not long after I moved into high school, this Sunday school teacher left his wife and three small girls for another woman. He had been having an affair for some time, and when his wife found out, he left. He moved to a small town nearby. I don't know exactly what happened, or how it happened, but less than a year later, he committed suicide.

• • •

But before all that, before anyone began to look at him askance, I sat in his classroom and prayed, and next door the adult Sunday school met to discuss the future of our church. The Evangelical Free church is a democratically organized church. The doctrinal statement reads, "We believe that Jesus Christ is Lord and Head of the Church and that every local church has the right, under Christ, to decide and govern its own affairs." Theoretically, it is unlike hierarchical Christian denominations that receive instruction and direction from church authorities; each Evangelical Free church is considered an autonomous congregation. And because of the democratic structure, it seems to place an emphasis on the human aspect of the church. The Evangelical Free church appears to embrace its earthly base, realizing that a church *is* people.

One of the things that the Evangelical Free members debate and vote on is pastor selection, which is where the tear that ended up ripping our church in half first began. Our pastor left the year before to take a different job and a new pastor was commissioned, Pastor Rick. Soon after, an associate pastor was added, Pastor Scott. In the end, half the church preferred one and the other half preferred the other, each thinking their man should be the head pastor or perhaps the only pastor. So the church began to divide, one camp for Rick, one camp for Scott.

• • •

The Geneseo Evangelical Free Church advocates adult baptism, full body submersion. At the front of the church behind the pulpit there is a false floor that can be removed to reveal a small pool, something like a hot tub. The pulpit can also be removed so that from the congregation there is a clear view of the tub. During baptismal services, candidates first stand in front of the tub and talk to the congregation, giving testimonials about how they came to God. They are dressed in white robes of light cotton, and most people wear their bathing suits underneath. After the testimonial the candidate walks to the tub, down its three steps, to the pastor who is waiting in the water. The pastor says some things and then dunks the person, raising them up like Jesus rose from the dead.

During their baptismal testimonies, time and time again, I watched people talk about the troubles and sins of their past and then about how God had made them new and whole, and how they had started on a new path. They told stories of drunkenness, lies, cheating, and abuse by others and by themselves. But, in the early morning sunlight, dressed in their white gowns, the possibility of sin seemed to have been extinguished. Their sins were expunged. Major catastrophes like cheating on your wife and leaving your family, could no longer happen, would no longer happen.

But, of course, they did, and they do.

It was confusing for me as a young adult moving from the world of childhood to the world of adulthood. Right and wrong were paramount. Those of us who were fourteen and fifteen and sixteen that summer were constantly being told about the dangers of lying, sex, gossip, drinking. We were hailed and rewarded when we avoided these vices by coming to an alternative post-school dance party or by taking a vow of chastity. Sin was to be warded off at every step using the sword of the Spirit, the Bible. And I was trying very hard to follow the rules. If I just kept heading down that devotional path, I could avoid sin and pain and all the things the adults around me regretted; in short, I could avoid being a human.

But I didn't want to avoid being human. I remember sitting outside church with my brother in my mom's Buick that summer, waiting for my mom to stop talking to people and come take us home. My brother would get the car key and put it in half a turn so the electric windows and radio worked. Ryan would sit in the driver's seat, and I'd sit in the passenger seat. We'd roll down the windows and listen to Casey Kasem's American Top Forty. I'd take off my shoes, white flats, revealing that my white tights were stained brown on the bottom from the leather inside the shoe. We wouldn't talk much. We'd listen to Whitney Houston and Rod Stewart and watch the cars pull out of the parking lot until we were one of the few cars left. It felt good to be out in the day, the car hot from the sun, my brother and I hungry and ready for lunch, the afternoon and week ahead of us. It felt good to be in this confined space with my brother, both of us on the same side, kids listening to the radio after church, feeling slightly rebellious, feeling like kids.

• • •

I think my brother was already disillusioned with our church. Two years earlier he had been a part of a weekly teenage boys Bible study led by the man who had served as interim pastor before Pastor Rick. Ryan was a freshman in high school and had become friends with some of the older guys in the group, which I think made him feel cool. After Ryan had been a part of the group for about a year, the interim pastor left our church. It was discovered that he had done something inappropriate with one of the boys in the group. What or to what extent I never found out. The man and his wife left Geneseo and moved to California. The teen group broke up. I've never talked to my brother about the incident, but I think more than anything he was hurt: his trust had been betrayed. He was just coming into his own sexuality, and I'm sure the thought of this man, whom he had trusted, violating someone he knew was shocking, perhaps terrifying. I have an image in my mind of my brother's face, pale and grave, and I always link that image to this time, to this event. The image contains a kind of setting of the jaw, reflecting a setting of the will and mind.

The scandal was shocking. Yet it seems this sort of thing happens again and again in churches. The pastor of a friend of mine left his wife for the youth leader in the church. The pastor and his wife had two small children who both have a rare disease, making them difficult to care for, and he just left one night, without any warning. Another friend of mine learned that her youth leaders were having an affair with each other. The same struggles come up over and over, in every church, in every era. Take for example the church split. At the very opening of his first letter to the Corinthians, Paul says "It has been reported to me by Chloe's people that there are quarrels among you, my brothers and sisters. What I mean is that each of you says, 'I belong to Paul,' or 'I belong to Apollos,' or 'I belong to Cephas,' or 'I belong to Christ.'" How much does this echo my own church's split: one says "I belong to Rick," another "I belong to Scott."

I don't think those outside of the church are ever as shocked as those in it. For those outside the church, it is almost expected or inevitable. It is the black side of the black and white, and there can't be one without the other, the flesh and the spirit, the good and the bad. Of course, in a secular sphere, such as television, one sees almost the opposite extreme—everyone will eventually cheat on their spouse, steal from their place of work, betray their friends. These things are to be expected. But it seems to me that both extremes are unnatural. We are human: we are black and white, we are flesh and spirit, we are good and bad.

• • •

When I think of church when I was a little girl, I picture sitting next to my mother during the service, leaning against her, her breath soft and warm as she asks me if I want a piece of candy. She pulls from her purse a small change pouch that holds mints, butterscotches, and cinnamon Trident gum. I take the butterscotch, which tastes like the cinnamon gum, having been kept in close quarters for so long. The butterscotch is slightly stale, and its outer coating is no longer hard. When I was a child, church was about stale candy and my mother; it was about the smell of the church basement and the gold carpet in the narthex. It is only as I aged that religion and God became ideas around which I felt I needed to organize my life and politics.

Church is translated from the Greek word *ecclesia*, which means assembly. It makes me think of the child's nursery rhyme where you clasp your hands together, fingers in, knuckles out, and say "Here is the church, here is the steeple, open the doors and see all the people," pointing your index fingers to make a steeple, then opening your hands to see all the people. All those wiggling fingers seem an accurate image to represent what church felt like for me as a child—walking into our church foyer with everyone towering above me talking and shaking hands, tall, tall Carl Brinkman bending down at the waist to tease me, Pat Hemminger in her wheelchair taking my hand in her own, so soft and delicate.

It is interesting to think about how this changes, how we grow up and the impression of church, of growing up in the church, shifts. For me, the path twists and turns during the times of turmoil in our church. I began to recognize the gap between what people were asking of me and what they were able to do themselves. The adults around me were only human, a bunch of wiggling, writhing fingers, humans trying to make it through, searching for the right path, wanting to be good people, wanting me to have a happy life, scared of pain and sin, scared of themselves and me and our shared humanity.

• • •

The church split brought out the worst in people—petty gossip and rumors, yelling and arguing during congregational meetings, storming out in a huff. In my mind, I lump the split together with my Sunday school teacher's suicide and the interim pastor's scandal. At first I thought they all happened close to the same time, but when I look back on the timeline I see that one happened a few years before, another a few years after. Why do I lump them all together? I'm not sure exactly, but I suppose it has to do with how each incident reinforced the imperfection and frailty of church people. Through each of these incidents, I realized that the people of the church were not able to live up to the standards they were asking me to live up to. At first this made me angry, but now it makes me sad. I worry that people who grow up in the church learn to deny their own humanity.

My mother talks confidently about the split now, over ten years later, able to posit the group that followed Scott as the "wrong" group and the group that stayed as "right." On the phone with my mother, I press her, saying that I thought she was more confused at the time of the split, and she says that yes, she was. She admits then that many of the people who were thinking of leaving were her friends. She tells me about how the week before Scott's last Sunday at church, someone came to the house in the evening to explain to her that a group had decided not to show up on Sunday and to leave the church for good. The woman tried to convince my mother to go with them. She spills out the names of the families that left our church in the split. They are names that I connect with my very earliest memories: the Tomshecks, the Junises, the Palmatiers. These were the founding members of the church, the people who had first guided my mother in her walk with God. For me, they are people I have not thought of in years, but suddenly as my mother says their names I see them before me: I kissed Josh Tomsheck when I was in the second grade, and Judy Junis taught me how to spin wool when we visited her house for a Super Bowl party. Just to hear my mother say these names is painful. I realize that these people not only walked out on the church, they walked out on our lives as well.

A church split. It is such a violent word, *split*. I see a piece of wood axed in half or the curtain of the temple torn in two. My aunt and uncle recently went through a church split—for many of the same reasons our church split: mainly disagreements about the direction of the church, the leadership of the church, and which members held the most power. They had raised their daughters in that church and had been extremely active in it, so it surprised me when they left. When they talk about the split, it is as if they experienced some kind of trauma—there is pain and bitterness and sadness. My cousin, Danna, is leaving her church, along with many of its other members, because the church lost its pastor and has been unable to replace him with someone Danna and her husband respond to. So off the members go, trudging over that cornfield of my daydream, trying to find a new home.

• • •

Now, when I am home, I accompany my mother to church. I recognize some of the faces, people who went through the split and stayed, along with my mother. But many of the members are new, people who joined the church after I left for college. Even the pastor is new; Rick has taken a post in New Jersey at a larger evangelical church. The new pastor is nothing like Rick, and I have to say I don't like him half as well, but the congregation seems to approve. But that doesn't mean all is settled in the church community. My mother still leads music, and recently there was a scandal because half of the congregation wanted to hire a full-time music leader, and the other half wanted to keep it on a weekly volunteer basis. The man they wanted to hire was a member of the church, and when he wasn't voted in, he left the church, along with his supporters.

It is hard for me even now to reconcile the expectations of church and the reality of being alive. Not long ago I was shopping with my mother and we went out to lunch together. Sitting at another table right across from us were two women who go to her church. I didn't recognize either of them; my mother couldn't remember their names. It was a Mexican restaurant, and we had been out shopping. I suggested to my mother that we should get margaritas, her favorite mixed drink. She leaned over and quietly explained that she would rather not, not in front of the ladies from church. Even my mother has a secret side.

I asked my brother about growing up in our church and what that had been like for him. He said, "I never really felt like I fit in at that church. I felt like everyone was always being fake-nice to each other on Sunday morning. I really didn't feel like they were my friends; they were just people to greet on Sunday. I found out after I left Geneseo that there are churches that are more relaxed than our church." He is now married to a woman who was raised Catholic. They had a huge wedding in her hometown Catholic church. They just had a baby girl, and I wonder if they will raise her in a church.

I am still wondering what it means to be myself and be spiritual. Sometimes I try to pray, late at night when I am unable to sleep, my bed hot from my body and me tossing and turning. It is hard not to pray in a rehearsed way, and I can feel myself perform a routine even in my most desperate moments: "Oh Lord, please help me do X or feel Y." So I try to sink back into myself, to a self that is unaware of church and religion, to a more primal self. I imagine God as the night sky, not a man or even a person, and then I try just to be me, to be real, to experience my humanity with God as a witness.

3

Going
Way
against the
Flow

by Anne Dayton

Recently, I lost my DC Talk CD. I freaked out. I searched high and low for it. I accused my husband of hiding it (he has this weird aversion to listening to bad Christian music). But he denied all wrongdoing, and in the interest of a peaceful home, I let it go. Still, I wanted it back. DC Talk may be fifteen years past their sell-by date, but their music is important in the history of my faith. Plus, that CD was practically brand new.

See, I didn't exactly grow up in a Christian home. My mom became a Christian shortly after I was born, but my dad didn't. My mom took my brothers and me to church in my early years, and I officially became a Christian when I was eight, when my Sunday school teacher told me I needed to accept Jesus into my heart. I was shocked. All along, I thought he'd always just been there. But I dutifully prayed the sinner's prayer, asked Jesus into my heart, and lamented all the wasted years when I could have been following God. I didn't really feel all that different, but I knew it was a good thing, especially since we stopped going to church soon after that.

Our church attendance had always been a little spotty anyway, since my dad wasn't especially supportive about the whole thing, leaving my mom to drag three unwilling children to learn silly songs

23

and play with a flannel board every week. Understandably, this got tiring. Despite my heartfelt devotion, even I knew Sunday school was lame. I wanted to stay home and play Nintendo, and my two brothers were even less willing to spend time away from their friends, Mario and Luigi. Plus, church meant dresses and tights. I would do anything to get out of wearing tights. Slowly, we started showing up on Sunday mornings less and less. My mom honestly tried her best to get us there, but for the sake of family harmony and her marriage, she let it slip sometimes. Months would pass between our guest appearances, and then we gave up altogether. At first, it was great—I could play Zelda all day!—but I would soon come to regret this.

Even without church, though, I was convinced that my Christianity defined me. I cleared out a section of my closet and set up a makeshift church, where I would read the Bible in secret and conduct my own worship services, complete with Communion. Obviously, I hadn't quite grasped the meaning of that ceremony, and I often had to make do with water since my mom didn't stock grape juice in the fridge. (It never occurred to me to use the wine we did have.) But even though it felt weird, I knew that Communion was what Christians were supposed to do, so I tried my best.

This secret style of worship continued comfortably until I hit junior high. The traumas of frizzy hair, zits, and puberty were enough to make any girl want to hide in the closet, but somehow I managed to make a friend at school. Lo and behold, she was a Christian! Her family went to a church across town, and she invited me to come to youth group with her. I was thrilled—a real church! With other people! And some of the people were cute boys!

I was hooked. With the fervency of a new believer, I threw myself into youth group. I started coming every Wednesday night and promptly developed a crush on one of the boys. I soon felt very comfortable there, but no matter how many weekend retreats and campouts I went on, I knew almost instinctually that I could never *quite* fit in. It didn't occur to me to wonder why believing in Jesus wasn't enough, because it was obvious. My parents didn't know their parents. I hadn't been in Sunday school with them since nursery. They all seemed to have this vast and secret knowledge of song lyrics—hymns as well as contemporary tunes—that I could never hope to acquire. The other kids were just different. Their families came to church every Sunday, had dutifully taken them to AWANA, and now took them to youth group every Wednesday. They listened to the "right music"—Michael W. Smith and Stephen Curtis Chapman and Amy Grant, and later Audio Adrenaline and the Newsboys—not Mariah Carey and Nirvana and Weezer. These girls weren't allowed to read *Seventeen* magazine, which I got at home, but they all had a subscription to *Brio*, the Christian pseudo-alternative. And they were all reading Robin Jones Gunn's Christy Miller series, advertised in *Brio* each month, instead of the romance novels I favored. In short, they had a carefully filtered world filled with positive influences and inspirational media that would lead them along the way everlasting. Instead, I had a family who watched PBS on Sunday mornings.

It was clear to me that these youth group kids had something I didn't, and I wanted it. All of it.

Mostly, I wanted a DC Talk tape. In those pre-iPod days, back when CDs were still cutting-edge, DC Talk was the epitome of cool among the youth group kids. The group's poppy R&B-inspired inspirational music was soulful and deep. We would sing their slower songs in worship on Wednesday nights, and most of my friends had DC Talk posters on their bedroom walls and albums in their stereos. And this was before they released the pivotal song "Jesus Freak" in my sophomore year of high school. The song exploded onto the Christian music charts and became the anthem for Christians of my generation, inspiring them to be bold and proud of their faith. *100 Greatest Songs in Christian Music* (where it ranks number two, just behind "Awesome God" by Rich Mullins) calls it "a hybrid of hard-edged, guitar-driven grunge rock and in-your-face Christian lyrics—with the occasional rap break thrown in for good measure."* I never quite managed to listen to the words, but I loved the tune, and I wanted it anyway.

I was proud of my faith. And I wanted everything I thought it was about. I was given a gift subscription to *Brio*, which only intensified my longing for the Christian books and music advertised in its

---

* Tori Taff and the editorial staff of CCM Magazine, *100 Greatest Songs of Christian Music: The Stories Behind the Music That Changed Our Lives Forever* (Nashville: Integrity, 2006), 6.

pages. I wanted someone to give me a True Love Waits ring. I craved one of those "Go against the Flow" T-shirts. (Remember those? They had the Christian fish swimming against a sea of secular fish.) I wanted to wear it to school and make a public declaration that I was *going against the flow*. Then everyone would know that I was a Christian.

But I never got any of these things. Mostly, I think, because I never bothered to ask. And to this day, I'm not really sure why. My parents are not selfish ogres, nor are they anti-church (my mom taught at a Christian school, for crying out loud). They never denied me much.

I guess it somehow didn't occur to me to ask my parents to buy these things for me. Part of my reticence was a shyness, a sense, probably developed during my days in my closet, that religion was a private affair, and that talking about it was deeply revealing and embarrassing, like talking about your bra size or getting your period. Even in church, I couldn't work up the courage to pray out loud; prayer was something I did in the quiet space of my mind. We rarely talked about God in my house. The one time my mom suggested I pray over a Thanksgiving dinner, I was so self-conscious I just shook my head and started eating.

I'm sure there was also a certain sense of guilt involved, as if embracing the Christian subculture was rejecting the mainstream world my family lived in, and thus, them. And I guess I thought having to ask my parents for Christian stuff in the first place was itself the problem. If mine had been the kind of family I thought I wanted, the kind who went to church every week and signed me up for youth group retreats before I even knew about them, they would have *known* what all the "cool" kids were wearing and reading and listening to. They would be trying to keep my cultural influences safely within the self-protective bubble of Christian culture all along.

Maybe this is how I ended up marrying a Baptist boy from Grand Rapids, Michigan, where there are more churches per capita than anywhere else in the country. He spent his childhood listening to Christian radio and watching Davey and Goliath videos, instead of the Beatles and bad sitcoms that ruled my house. His family went to church on Wednesday night and twice on Sunday. They handed out tracts and never touched alcohol. The license-plate holder on his parents' car said "I Love AWANA" (a fact that effectively ended his dating life in high school when they wouldn't let him take it off). He was so cool, he actually *went* to a DC Talk concert in high school. He had the family I wanted.

Though he often refers to his early church experience with a certain amount of derision, I don't think he would trade these formative days for anything. He was taught several theological points he now disagrees with, but he also learned about the deep and abiding love of God. The habits that he now looks back on as legalism also showed him the value of diligence and spiritual discipline. Though he insists he can only handle one church service per week, he also wants to become actively involved in whatever church we join. The lessons instilled in him as a child have shaped who he is today, and for that I have to thank his family and their church.

But even though I was stuck with parents who drank wine with dinner and believed in science (my dad has a PhD in astrophysics), they allowed me space to be who I wanted, and they tried to encourage a healthy balance between my "church things" and the rest of my world. In other words, they were always trying to get me to lighten up. At one point they asked me to stop bringing my Bible to school every day because it made people think I was a freak. But they also never had to worry about me staying out too late on a Saturday night or drinking or smoking or being alone with a boy. I like to think that I was every Christian parent's dream—I just didn't have the right kind of parents.

When I got my driver's license, the first thing I did was slap a fish decal on the car. I was finally able to drive myself to church. I joined a youth group close to my house and started attending every event they hosted. I volunteered for the children's ministry. I volunteered for VBS. I volunteered for nursery duty. I was finally able to act like I really belonged. I threw away all my secular CDs, although I wasn't cool enough to actually own very many. Over the summers, I got a job as a lifeguard and used my money to buy Jars of Clay and Newsboys tapes. My dad asked me not to play them around him, wisely assessing them as atonal and repetitive.

It wasn't until college that I began to find the culture I had adopted a little . . . narrow. I was three thousand miles away from home, and I surrounded myself with Christian friends and influences. And it was good, for a while. But as I saw more of the world and met many intelligent, fascinating people from all walks of life, I started to wonder if you really had to embrace Christian culture—all of it—to be a worthy Christian.

Many of my contemporaries were dealing with the same questions. College is a time when you're supposed to refocus your view of the world. My Christian friends were questioning the narrowness of the culture they had been brought up in, and many started rebelling against the parents who had sheltered them in the bubble of Christian pop culture for so long. I, on the other hand, was looking at the choices I had made and wondering if, maybe, my parents might have been right all along.

I was twenty-five when I finally bought my DC Talk CD (unsure of which album to buy after so many years, I went for their greatest hits). I lived in New York and had started attending a church full of artists and hipsters. Most of them had grown up in the bubble, and though they loved the Lord, they were completely turned off by the culture that went along with it. We drank lots of wine and listened to indie rock and laughed at the youth groups who came to New York on short-term mission trips. I worked for a major publishing company, successfully passing myself off as a normal human being despite the fact that I happened to go to church. Religion-bashing was a hobby for many of my work friends. I would often join in. It was cool to be cynical. Jesus bobble-head dolls were all the rage, and the movie *Saved!* had just come out, which had my friends and me rolling in the aisles laughing at the Christian hypocrisy we knew so well. It was suddenly very cool to know the names of obscure Bible characters and to be able to quote all the naughty verses in the Bible. I was single, I had moved into a tiny studio apartment, and I was on my own, really on my own, for the first time. Finally, I could come to my faith on my own terms and look at what I had been clinging to.

And I realized that for all those years I prayed all alone in my dark little closet, what I really wanted was community. When I saw a Christian T-shirt, I saw a kid whose family believed that God's love was worth advertising. When I heard a new Audio Adrenaline tape, I heard a family's hope for their child. When I desperately wanted books where the characters were all Christian, I was really grasping for a world where I could actually live this way.

And finally, I saw that the very fact that I was longing for these things had made me a part of it all along. Even though I felt like an outsider because I didn't have the right things, I had always had the one thing that made me belong. Somewhere along the line, I had bought into the idea, so pervasive in evangelical culture, that reading the right books and listening to the right music will make you ("inspire you to be") a better Christian. Somehow, I had confused the trappings of faith with faith itself.

So I finally bought my DC Talk album. I would blast "Jesus Freak" from my cubicle at work because I could laugh with the cool kids who knew all the words. I learned to appreciate, as my dad had pointed out a decade before, the atrocious lyrics of nineties Christian rock. (Exhibit A: "People say I'm strange, does it make me a stranger, that my best friend was born in a manger?" This is truly craptastic.) Now, it's funny and ironic to know all the words to DC Talk's song "What if I Stumble?" and to pull them out at inappropriate times (for instance, when you're hiking up a mountain and your friend is afraid of heights), but when I listen to "I Wish We'd All Been Ready," it's only partly ironic.

Multnomah Publishers recently re-released the Christy Miller series I so coveted as a pre-teen, and I've been devouring them. They're quick easy reads, filled with three of my favorite things—sunshine, romance, and teenage angst. The things that make me roll my eyes now (Christy's thoughts on trying out for cheerleading: "God, I want to do this cheerleading thing for you . . . If I become a cheerleader, people will look up to me and respect me. That will give me a better chance to tell them that I'm a Christian and maybe to invite them to church with me or something") are exactly the sections I know would have inspired me when I was young. Naïve assurances to Christy that innocence is what makes a girl sexy make me skeptical about the author's real message, and also make me wonder when I became so jaded.

I've scoured the Internet, but I can't find a "Go against the Flow" T-shirt anywhere. I never did get a True Love Waits ring, but now I wear a wedding ring; in a way, they amount to sort of the same thing.

Now that I'm an adult, I can embrace the things I wanted as a child, secure in the knowledge that Christianity is about much more than wearing cool shirts. The love of Christ that sustained me through the years I felt alone and out of place is also the bond that included me in the fellowship of believers all along.

• • •

A few months after my CD went missing, I had a revelation. Around the time it was lost, our car had been broken into, and our radio, along with all the CDs in the glove compartment, were stolen (sigh— we live in Brooklyn, what can you do?). I think the thief stole my DC Talk CD. The reason it was in the glove compartment remains, to this day, unclear. My husband swears he grabbed it accidentally, but I suspect that he, too, secretly likes to be reminded of his youth group days every now and then.

And for some reason, it gives me immense pleasure to imagine how the thief reacted when he discovered the nature of his loot. I like to imagine some thug, rockin' out to "Jesus Freak." Who knows? Maybe he'll even listen to the words.

4

Family
Time

by Carla-Elaine Johnson

My family's mix of religious identity contributed heavily to my spiritual restlessness—the African Methodist Episcopal church, deeply connected to the community of 1930s South Baltimore, on my mother's side, and a Baptist faith born in the heart of southern Virginia on my father's. My parents' marriage united both branches of Christianity without much conflict in our family.

My parents probably compromised in terms of how to raise a child to reflect both Methodist and Baptist roots. In the end, like in so many families, my mother took the lead in choosing my religious education. Although my father later would embrace the Baptist faith anew at City Temple Baptist Church, when I was born he did not insist that I be baptized in his faith. My mother arranged for the minister from Ebenezer AME Church to visit their tiny apartment in West Baltimore one afternoon. The minister baptized me in the African Methodist Episcopal faith that same day.

Practicality and the desire to provide a strong educational background influenced my parents' choices. My mother enrolled me in Wayland Baptist Nursery School, which I attended from age two until age five. Wayland Baptist provided a safe, nurturing environment with a religious focus. The educational curriculum focused on colors, numbers, and personal information. I left knowing how to spell my name, how to write my home telephone number, and how to say where I lived.

Just before my fifth birthday, my parents decided to move from Eldorado Avenue in the West Baltimore Liberty Heights neighborhood, further east, to Melville Avenue in a neighborhood called Waverly. My parents' house on Melville Avenue stood just over a block away from Memorial Stadium. An elementary school was just around the corner.

My mother disapproved of the educational methods of the nearby elementary school. She noticed that children came home with little to no homework. So instead of sending me to the public school, my parents sent me to Saint Cecilia's, a parochial school run by the Oblate Sisters, an order of African-American nuns. I vaguely remembered an interview with Sister Elizabeth, a light-skinned nun with black hair and a slender figure. Later, my mother would tell me how the secretary and my future babysitter, Mrs. Grey, had persuaded Sister Elizabeth to admit a scrawny kid from the other side of town.

As a child and as an adult, I always considered my childhood to be Christian fundamentalist, though looking back, I was sure most true fundamentalist parents would have home-schooled me or sent me to public school. Although my parents sent me to parochial school, they still insisted on religious education in their own respective denominations of Christianity. My parents and grandparents presented faith as the glue that held the world together in the most positive sense.

Because faith was the glue that held the world together, good Christian black children never failed to show up at church unless they had fallen ill. Even when we drove down to visit Cousin Bessie and my father's relatives in Virginia, we still went to church.

On one visit, from what I recall, we drove down to Suffolk on a warm August night. My parents pulled the car into my cousin's driveway, around eight o' clock or so in the evening. The dirt road filled with four or five houses seemed to have risen out of the middle of a few fields. The trip took forever. I hated the potholes and the barely visible white signs. I was glad my father knew the way. My butt stuck to the warm vinyl seats. I just wanted to get out of the hot car. Every window was open, but that didn't stop the itchy feeling, as mosquitoes bit through the light cotton shirt and shorts I wore. Sweat poured down my face and arms, but I knew better than to ask for air conditioning. My father never turned on the air conditioning in the car. He believed it was a luxury.

After we got out of the car, my father grabbed my arm. "Mind your manners," Dad said. "Don't ask Cousin Bessie about food. We'll feed you later."

Cousin Bessie followed the rules of traditional hospitality. If a child asked for food, then she would take whatever she had to give. At the time, no one told me that my cousins barely had enough to eat. In Cousin Bessie's house, she always welcomed strangers as guests.

So that evening, in spite of my father's protests, Cousin Bessie insisted on making dessert. She took a bit of what looked like a plain sheet cake to the kitchen and returned with the top and middle parts slathered with a thick grape jelly. I had never had jelly cake before. The gooey grape mess got all over my mouth, but I didn't care.

After a few hours of catching up with news of weddings, funerals, and babies, my father prepared to leave. My dad had made reservations at the local motel.

"Charlie"—Cousin Bessie never called my father by his legal name, only his family nickname—"there's plenty of room here. Don't go anywhere," she added.

Cousin Bessie lived on the Baptist traveling-preacher circuit, just outside Suffolk. The preacher served Cousin Bessie's church every second and fourth Sunday, unless there was a special wedding or funeral. This type of arrangement was normal for this part of rural Virginia.

Sunday morning dawned bright. Cousin Bessie served pancakes with corn syrup. My mother dressed me in a pink dress, with patent leather black shoes. She braided my hair into three thick plaits, with pink barrettes on the ends of the plaits.

"Mind yourself," my mother reminded me. I viewed church as mandatory, but not always enjoyable. "And leave your book here," she added with a sigh. I loved to read, but Judy Blume's *Forever* was not on the preferred religious book list. This time my mother didn't go to church, but stayed at home with Cousin Bessie who looked a bit tired.

My father dropped my cousins and me off at Sunday school. We arrived just before nine, for Sunday school—the regular service started at eleven. I tried not to wiggle about in my seat, but by eleven thirty, my patent leather shoes pinched my toes and my stockings itched in the warm church. I wanted to take off my shoes, but I knew my father would have yelled at me. I learned my first lesson in feminine fashion: in church, the goal was to look good.

What I loved about the service was singing the hymns with the congregation. This was the first time I heard an extended version of the traditional gospel tune "O Happy Day." It was my favorite gospel tune. Later I would find out that the tune was a traditional call-and-response melody, similar to the blues:

> Oh happy day! (Oh happy day!)
> Oh happy day! (Oh happy day!)
> When Jesus washed, (When Jesus washed)
> Oh, when he washed (When Jesus washed)
> Oh, when he washed (When Jesus washed)
> He washed my sins away.

On that particular morning, "Oh Happy Day" lasted at least ten minutes. Everyone around me sang something, even if it came out as a mumbled noise. My stomach rumbled. I squeezed my butt cheeks together, hoping it would make me forget my hunger. I pushed the edges of my pink dress towards the end of the pew. I wondered if anyone would notice if I slid to the floor and tried to crawl out. Just when I thought my stomach could not rumble any more, the service ended. My father walked towards the front doors. The smell of ham, collard greens, and baked fish filled the air. I ran to my father and tugged on his hand.

"So this is your little girl?" an older woman in a bright orange hat asked.

"Yes," my father replied. My father pinched my hand slightly. I looked at the woman and smiled.

"Well, best get some food in her. We'll see you around four then?"

My father smiled. "I'll be here."

I tried to catch my father's eye. What did he mean about coming back at four? I wondered why one service was not enough. What I didn't know then was that this church was more traditional than the ones back home. We never had two services in the afternoon, but in these churches, folks took a break for supper, then came back for another service before dinner.

Cousin Bessie's church exemplified what my family called a "holy and sanctified" church. Women wore black thick-soled shoes called "stomping shoes." The women stood whenever the spirit moved them. They called the side-to-side rhythmic foot pattern "stomping." At a holy and sanctified church, people danced in ecstasy and stood on their feet for long periods. They praised Jesus as Lord and Savior. That morning, every now and then, someone would stand up and start dancing in place, as though unaware of their surroundings. My father explained that these women were "getting happy."

Older women in white nursing uniforms stood along the side of the wall. Each woman wore a pair of short white gloves. Tiny heart shaped medals hanging from purple or white ribbons decorated the left breast pockets of their uniforms. My father explained that these women comforted those who fainted or "fell out" during the service. My mother later added that usually people fell out during funerals or just after turning over their lives to Jesus.

For the first time, I understood how religiously liberal my parents had raised me. My northern upbringing with my exposure to atheist, Catholic, Jewish, Hindu, and other religious traditions contradicted what I saw during that brief visit to Suffolk. I belonged because of my family ties, the color of my skin, and the religion of my parents. But inside, I did not feel that I truly belonged. Instead, I watched the praise and worship as an outsider, the child who longed to join in the revelry yet remained on the sidelines.

By age nine I suspected that Christianity held no place for me, a child who talked to God directly, rather than speaking through Jesus. As a child, I wondered, why was belief in Jesus more important than just direct prayer to God? Why was I not a good little girl if I confessed that I really didn't want to pray just to Jesus? Insufficient responses from adults in my life led to a sense of unease. This restlessness launched my spiritual journey away from Christianity.

My parents' choices also influenced my future religious path. Had they chosen the strict black Baptist tradition of my father's parents, I would have explored the life of the ministry under the revival tent at best. But when they chose to give me the best education they could afford, they allowed me to see the world beyond the confines of traditional black Baptist or Methodist religious life.

• • •

The structure of the Baptist church wrapped family life as tightly as the cord that bound the legs of the turkey my father cooked for family dinners. Food and faith marked the holidays in my family, and no day exemplified this more than Thanksgiving. My fourteenth Thanksgiving fed my sense of spiritual disconnect. At fourteen, I had begun to equate my faith with my race. For the first time, I saw that a good and respected black person believed in Jesus, went to church weekly, worked hard for the family, and took care of children. I grasped my religious identity, in part, from the strength of grandparents who founded Emmanuel Baptist Church. My parents only added to this structure.

My father, a round-faced, balding man with a salt-and-pepper moustache who wore reading glasses more often than not, slid the turkey into the oven around seven in the morning. At ten, a mouthwatering aroma permeated kitchen and hallway, when my father basted the turkey and slid it back into the oven. Around eleven he looked at me with a grin.

"Ready to make some biscuits?" he asked.

"Yep," I said.

Dad mixed flour and water in a bowl, while I pulled some cheddar cheese out of the refrigerator. Dad called these "Depression-era" biscuits, because my grandparents made them during the Depression when they weren't able to afford more than flour and water.

By noon, my parents and I bustled about the house. I cleaned the bathrooms and vacuumed the hall carpet. My father turned on the 1964 Magnavox brown stereo hi-fi system in the living room. The sonorous tones of "O Mary, Don't You Weep" filled the room. My parents only permitted gospel music or classical music on Sundays and holidays. Birds played by the water dish on the back deck.

The dinner started as it did every Thanksgiving. Everyone in the household gathered in a circle, we held hands, and my grandmother prayed aloud. She asked for blessings over the food, the household, and all those in it. She asked God to grant all present the knowledge and the love of Jesus.

I dared not lift my gaze from the floor. My stomach began to rumble. I bit back one giggle, then another. My throat rattled with a choking sound. I felt the laughter bubble up in my throat, and I tried to fight it. My grandmother's prayer was too long for me. I did not understand the religious fervor that guided her words and her prayers. I did not comprehend the ways of prayer or see how the divine spoke through my grandmother or the women in Cousin Bessie's church.

I listened to my grandmother's repeated thanks for being saved by the blood of Christ and how her life became richer because of Jesus's presence in it. I closed my eyes and bit my lip. The laughter was closer, just behind my lips. I pressed my tongue to the roof of my mouth. I tasted the blood as my teeth bit the edge of my lower lip. My head rolled slightly from side to side as I heard my grandmother's voice rumble in my ears. I did not hear the shaking in her voice, just the fear in my gut that I'd let the laugh out. I did not hear the tears in her voice, only silence that grew around her voice.

My stomach growled, and I bit back more laughter. Tears squeezed past my closed eyelids. I knew at least fifteen minutes had passed since my grandmother began the blessing. A cousin nudged me in the side. I raised my head slowly. I silently gave thanks for not passing out with laughter during the actual prayer. I felt a bit ashamed, though, as though I missed something precious in those moments. At the time, I thought the best prayers were quick: "Lord, thanks for this food. Let's eat." Later, I would realize that my grandmother demonstrated her connection with the divine in clear, honest, and simple ways. She embraced her faith and who she was as a person. After the meal, I cleared the table. My grandfather pulled out a cassette tape player and a few tapes. One of my aunts, my grandmother, and a few cousins joined my grandfather and me at the dining room table.

"Larry's trial sermon," he announced proudly. Cousin Larry had studied to be a preacher in the African Methodist Episcopal tradition. My grandfather explained how the trial sermon was a type of final exam.

The tape played for twenty minutes. I grew bored and snuck downstairs.

Cousin Larry stood in the corner. I seldom saw him at family dinners due to his heavy work schedule. Larry was fifteen years older than me, and I thought he was the epitome of a good-looking black male. He wore his hair in a short, neat afro. I'd had a crush on Larry at age eight, but that had quickly passed.

Larry stopped me to ask me about school, my homework, and boys. I confessed that French was hard, but school was okay. I admitted that I liked a guy named David who attended Cardinal Gibbons, a male parochial high school across town.

"Good, good." Larry sounded pleased.

"Have you considered Christ lately?" Larry asked, his voice rather low key. It was always pitched low, like he should have been a jazz singer or a disc jockey, not my cousin who was trying to save souls. I hadn't suspected that he would try to keep me Christian. Perhaps he could sense that my heart strayed from traditional Baptist and AME beliefs. By that time, I believed that religion was a choice and not all religion had to be the same type or the same practice to feel love from the same God.

I also knew that saying any of this openly in my family would be the same as if I announced that I was an atheist.

I shrugged, hoping he would leave me alone. This worked well with strangers but not with family. It certainly didn't work well with a missionary in the family.

"Maybe you should you know," Larry continued, oblivious to my discomfort, "without Christ you wouldn't be here. He makes all things possible."

I politely wanted to remind him that in my opinion there was the whole Jesus thing and then the God thing. I still hadn't figured out why Jesus was so important to reach God. Neither Catholic nuns nor weekly church sermons had ever convinced me that Jesus was necessary to reach God.

"Here." He handed me a small three by five inch blue booklet. He turned it over in my hand. He showed me the list of reasons to consider Christ as an option for my life. I closed my eyes. I didn't know whether to laugh or cry.

I stared at this pamphlet, this tract. Usually strangers used these booklets to sell me their religious beliefs. It reminded me of the tiny *Watchtower* brochures that Jehovah's Witnesses passed out on Saturday mornings in our neighborhood. On his Saturdays off, my father welcomed such groups into our home. He clearly enjoyed religious debate. But I did not.

"Um, thanks." I fidgeted in place.

"Just think about it. And let's talk." Larry gave me a smile that said he knew I would agree with him, once I thought it over.

I nodded and raced back upstairs to my room. My hands shook. It was the first time anyone confronted me about my religious choices.

Larry's comments hadn't offended me directly. Like others on my father's side of the family, Larry had declared himself a missionary of Christ. I knew that such missionaries were compelled to reach out to anyone not familiar with Christ. With the family, the missionary made sure that the word had not been forgotten.

As I sat on my bed, I knew that this conversation was more than just a creepy encounter with an older cousin. This particular Thanksgiving marked the first time that I questioned whether my grandparents' and cousins' fundamentalist Christian beliefs were ones that appealed to me. While I did not consider myself to be anything but a Christian at this point in my life, I also knew that the template of a good Christian life would never appeal to me. I liked the services, but not the holier-than-thou attitude of those in my family towards those who were not saved.

That one conversation with Larry reignited my sense of spiritual restlessness. It was just one moment of many that sparked my spiritual journey. Faith kept me looking beyond fundamentalist Christianity for the answer to my internal beliefs. This led me to explore Judaism and eventually Hellenic Orthodoxy. I embraced the Hellenic Orthodox religion, only to find that it was a mirror of the praise-and-worship style of the very Baptist fundamentalist church of my childhood. The irony did not escape me then that I might run from the faith of my fathers only to return in a different manner later.

On that Thanksgiving, I realized that my faith was a private act, not a public avowal. This contrasted with the Christianity of my grandparents and my cousins. Their Christianity emphasized a public expression of faith as essential to true Christianity. At fourteen, spiritual contentment meant being able to dance with friends or listen to the music I loved. I had no desire to proselytize or spread the word. I figured that attraction to a faith was good enough. My life spoke for my faith.

My family gave me wings, in the form of a loving, caring, strong faith. Those same wings allowed me to understand that not everyone has to be beneath the same tent to enjoy the view.

Enter into
His Gates with
Thanksgiving

WORSHIP

5

Keep the
Feast

by Nicole Sheets

It is the night before Easter, and I've let a man I love borrow my car to visit an art show without me. It is Saturday night, Holy Saturday, and I have baked brownies for the party at Christ Church. I don't belong to this church. For now, I'm only casually Episcopal, but a week ago I felt that I should sign the list for baked goods, that I should make some kind of commitment. The man with my car, on the way to Baltimore, would be proud to know I made up my mind, at least, on this small scale.

It is Easter, and I'm wearing sneakers, suede sneakers faded mute blue. Christ Church is a dressy church, and the Great Vigil of Easter is perhaps the biggest shebang of the year. I have never worn sneakers to this church before and am puzzled, when I pull into the parking lot in the man's rattling Toyota, that I followed a whim in wearing them. Toting my brownies I realize my mistake: the faithful are dressed to the nines.

In the room used for Sunday morning coffee hour, the vigil-keepers circle up, holding candles, unlit, with little paper shields like stiff skirts to catch the wax. Families cluster, the single and widowed link together with friends, while I nudge my way into an outer ring of God's people, uneasy about my shoes, trying to disguise the fact— as if the vigil were a cocktail party—that I am alone.

The thurifer walks down the aisle ahead of the priest and shakes incense from a censer like a small, gaudy light fixture, coating our prayers unto God. In the rosy light of the spring evening, we walk in silence to the front of the church. Traffic passes. A tree in blossom suggests a pointillist painting of a tree. A girl on a bike tilts her head toward us, then pedals faster. We must look awfully Old Testament, I think, like a small tribe washed in wonder as we shuffle by the paschal fire burning on the church's front steps, tipping our wicks to Christ's flame.

The lights inside are dim, but the church is not dark. April dusk gives way reluctantly. Even the darkest hours of Christendom are somehow light-limned. The altar glares naked; the cross is gone, God having died.

Yesterday at noon, during the Good Friday service, a jackhammer beat a street corner by the church. Sunlight warmed the windows. We prayed for ministers; for congregations; for the church triumphant serving Christ in heaven; for the church militant, fighting the good fight in real time. We prayed *for those whose faith is known to God alone.* I liked this effort to cover all the bases. Good Friday pares away the music and the Eucharist. No table spreads before us. No wedding feast. Our bridegroom has left us, left us at the altar, and all we do is watch for love's return.

• • •

I maneuver my little flame, shuffling between hymnal and prayer book as best I can to keep pace with the liturgy. The readings are lengthy and somehow distant, these same stories that have been with me from the faintest pinprick of memory. They're sort of God's greatest hits, a litany of his most shining moments of beauty and deliverance. These stories are pure cinema. Cue the rainbow offering its backbend of a covenant, pulled taut where each end kisses the transformed ground. Or perhaps a crane shot, high above the Red Sea, of the Hebrew millions shuffling past walls of water, the dust cloud of a doomed Pharaoh hot on the chase. Or simply the black screen of existence, the void before God's emphatic word, which slowly fades into light layered thick with water, trees, flesh.

Listening to the lilt and drone of the lineup of lectors, I wonder how much I trust these stories. Their weirdness has occurred to

me before. This is not panic, not by a long shot. But I have years
of Sunday school flannelgraph Christs to sift through, an oddly
Caucasian Savior, smiling in profile, as he balances a child on his left
knee or reaches for a blind man. I liked to touch the fuzzy flannelgraph board, to move the Sunday school lesson characters like paper
dolls. This Christ of my childhood, this paper Savior, opened these
stories to me before I could digest the words.

Our church is full of symbols, a priest assured me. I ask my literature students about symbols all the time. *Why the fence around
Dmitry's lover's house? And why is the ocean gold?* I want them to give
me a truckload of possible meanings because I want them to understand that an image's openness is its power. And so what do I make of
God's symbols: the water, the earth, the blood, the bread? Why the
pillar of cloud leading Israel by day, and at night, a pillar of fire?

The windows at Christ Church are stained-glass Bible tableaux.
In the chancel window, Christ sits kingly, his holy hand lifted in
peace. And every Sunday we echo his gesture, passing the *peace of
the Lord* to our neighbors in the pews. I'm glad that if I only get to
tell my neighbor one thing, that thing is *peace*. A time of greeting
in the middle of the church service is nothing new to me. In the
church where I grew up, while the choir sashayed from the choir
loft to their seats among the congregation, people would make the
rounds of the sanctuary, shaking hands with old friends and visitors.
Handshaking is about balance, really, between the limp fish shake
and the bone-crushing vise. Perhaps someday I'll graduate to the
two-handed shake that a spry nun once gave me at a soup kitchen,
her hands cupped around my own with a gentle press, as though
listening to me was all she wanted to do.

In my early days of Sunday school in the Baptist church, Lenora,
who even in my childhood was already an old woman, walked
through the sanctuary to my parents and me and asked if I'd like to
join the children in the choir. My parents, in their mid-thirties, had
decided to start attending church again, and that Sunday we were
trying on the small Baptist congregation about fifteen minutes from
our house. I took Lenora's grandmotherly hand and tottered after
her to a room beside the sanctuary where children had lined up.
I squeezed in somewhere near the back, not particularly unnerved

that I didn't know any of these children nor any of their songs. Our line snaked to the choir loft during *Boys and girls for Jesus, this our earnest prayer*, the opening melody, until everyone found their place. I stood and smiled in my red dress. I liked standing up front with these children, singing the catchy songs with hand motions. *The wise man built his house upon the rock, the wise man built his house upon the rock.* My arms extended overhead, my fingertips meeting at an angle like a peaked roof, made the *house*. Two fists, one pounding on the other, for the *rock*. My parents smiled, thinking me brave, watching me make up the words.

• • •

The Easter Vigil this year includes two baptisms, two infants with their stylish families in tow. At the back of the church, the priest touches one of the infants with water, and even from across the sanctuary I see the baby's fine, wild hair on end. It is a family's celebration, the parents and godparents pledging to guide their children to renounce Satan and turn to Christ. My mind drifts to my family back home. I have never passed an Easter without them, and now I second-guess why I was so adamant to stay here for the resurrection, to celebrate my Lover's return in Christ Church. These families are strangers to me, and it's hard for me to share in their joy.

• • •

In the photograph of my baptism I teeter between my bearded dad and Pastor Plybon waist-deep in the sea-green baptistery of the church's fellowship hall. Dad reaches his hand to pull me up from the water, intent on rescuing me from the symbolic death and burial, raising me to new life. My eyes are still closed. My whole family showed up, my aunt Jeanne wearing her slacks even though mom told her we're a skirt-wearing church. I was six, but old enough in this church to make my own profession of faith. I had already accepted Christ as my personal Savior, I told Pastor Plybon and the church. Baptism was just a symbol, a picture of obedience to Christ, he reminded the congregation. The water only made you wet, not saved. This water was on the cool side of lukewarm. It was winter. After the baptism, my mom helped me peel out of my wet, holy clothes and asked me to stand still for the hairdryer. My wet feet left prints on the concrete floor.

My parents and I joined the Baptist church where I'd first sung in the choir. My Methodist mother was surprised by the grip of the Baptist church, surprised that she could feel so at home among people who shouted *Amen* and *Glory* during the worship service, who lifted holy hands to God while singing, who stood up to testify of God's goodness, sometimes weeping. My dad, a Baptist all his life, must have felt he was simply coming home. Nana and Papa, Mom's parents, thought Mom and Dad were fanatics, driving out to church twice on Sundays and again on Wednesdays. My constant worry about sinning they chalked up to the Baptist penchant for hellfire preaching. From those early days I often asked permission for everything, to the point of absurdity, wanting to be as sure as possible that I was in the right. Really, though, it had little to do with denomination and much to do with temperament. I still compulsively want the okay.

• • •

The Easter Vigil started at dusk and now it's almost eleven. After the baptisms, we have finished with darkness. The readings are over; Christ is back, the house lights on. Incense thickens. The rector readies the Eucharist. The novelty of this church has gone stale in my mind. The liturgy is fresh to me, something I've come to only in my adulthood. But near the end of this vigil, I don't have the energy for newness, and I long for a familiar face, for someone I can touch to fill the pew beside me. I want to bolt out the door and breathe. I'm not thinking about how wonderful it is that the Savior has come back to us for another year. The church's vaulted ceiling closes in, the priest's white-robed figure distends awfully like something by El Greco, the light bears down hard, the hymn as unfamiliar as the faces.

I have put out my light and want to extinguish this vigil altogether. Staying for the party afterwards is out of the question. I figure I will cry on the way home, upset that I have to do Easter clumsily by myself, that I have chosen to spend Easter away from my family, and that the man with my car has chosen to spend it away from me. But first, the choir sings and my body joins the line for Holy Communion. At least in this unsure moment, ritual holds out a perch, a tenuous twig, for the mind to light upon. In my loneliness, in my panic, there's still the Eucharist. *It's like lovemaking*, a priest will tell me later. The early parts of the liturgy, the readings and prayers, are lovers' light talk, getting acquainted, or re-acquainted, wooing. The Eucharist calls forth the Body—we are kneeling, open-palmed, to receive the Body. Taking, eating, remembering—this is why we come. And after, we go. In our mouths the taste of our Lover.

Not only is Christ back, but he is consumed, consummated. *Christ our Passover is sacrificed for us; therefore let us keep the feast.* We sing this. We have been singing and keeping this feast for centuries. The bread, broken, sweet to the taste, is placed in my cupped palms. One Sunday a priest addressed me by name as he administered the bread. *Nicole, the body of Christ, the bread of heaven*, and I thought I might weep, scooping this manna meant for me.

I think of the Sunday school paper Jesus, the stone rolled away at his resurrection, the orb of the tomb's emptiness blank like a vacant eyeball. A preacher told me that Christ's corpse had been wrapped in linen, and that after he rose from the dead, the women found that linen folded in the manner of one who will return to finish his meal, like this meal at which we wait for his reappearing. My mind reaches back to December's nativity, the baby Christ mummied up in those swaddling clothes meant for the dead, and overhead, the star's pulsing. He's born in Bethlehem, the city of bread, a divine loaf destined to be broken.

In this Communion the chalice of wine, like a silver bell, tips toward my mouth. Many mouths taste the wine. As I kneel there, in Christ Church, a mural of angels looking on, the wine warms me. To drink the blood of one's Beloved strangely mixes metaphors, a gory intimacy. I feel the tingle of the wine down my throat and imagine something holy entering in, washing the innermost parts. It took time for me to get used to walking up to the altar for Communion. In the Baptist church, Communion is brought to you in your seat; here, you have to come and get it. It's more public as we stride down the aisle toward our Lover, ready to receive him. It's still a little awkward for me, and I don't feel ceremonious enough. I linger just a moment at the altar, maybe look up at a painted angel, and think of the body of Christ. *Though we are many,* a priest prays, *we are one Bread.*

There is a closeness and even a messiness in the common cup, a different relationship to the elements than what's allowed by the sterile, individual cups I grew up with. There is beauty in this wide-mouth chalice. It's fitting that our lips move in the same prayers and drink the same wine. In the Episcopal church, I have found there are *dippers,* those who touch the bread to the wine and eat the wet morsel, and *sippers,* who take wine straight from the vessel, *the blood of Christ, the cup of salvation.* My mother, accustomed to small plastic Communion cups of grape juice, was scandalized when I told her about the communal chalice and revealed that I am, definitely, a sipper.

• • •

Now it is Easter Sunday and I am alone, but wearing the right shoes. The church seems choked with people and light. I'm almost late, I who will likely be late for my own wedding, so I slip into an empty space beside a row of someone's squirmy grandchildren. The grand-children color the service leaflet. They kick their feet. They look at the people behind them and crouch by the kneeling bench. Perhaps this is wrong, but part of what draws me to this church is the anonymity it affords me. One older woman invited me to her house once for dinner, where I ate tender roast with her and her husband beneath a friendly chandelier. She has taken me by the arm during coffee hour, that blessed Episcopal tradition, to introduce me to people in the church. I'm learning names, but even so, I don't feel obligated to small-talk on my way out of church. No one knows my story. It's not a cold, stiff distance. I feel welcomed, but not pressured.

The church where I grew up is like a family, a body of people who've seen me run the gauntlet of childhood and adolescence. That church *is* a family, with all the misunderstandings and comforts. I haven't attended my parents' church regularly since I moved away for college, but when I'm back for a visit, the parishioners want to know how I am, what I'm up to. I haven't defined myself as an adult there; in the twice-a-year small talk, I don't feel like discussing the moves I've made within my faith since my days in their high school youth group. In that church I've played the Virgin at Christmas, I've felt the Spirit move and have stood to testify, I've sung in the choir. The first time I played the piano, an old upright, in church was at Christmastime. I hadn't practiced "O Little Town of Bethlehem" enough, and it was my turn in the program. I approached the piano, shaky, and sat in the halo of the dumpy florescent light resting above the music stand. I plodded through, aware of the audience I couldn't see. I wanted to slink out of the church. Turning around on the piano bench, I remember Mrs. White, my friend Ashley's mother, looking on, a kind woman who'd taught me in vacation Bible school, her body frail that winter from bone cancer. The next Christmas would come without her.

• • •

It is Easter Sunday, and I'm thinking about these children in church, about having been a child in church. What do they mean, these children? What are they symbols of as they clamber up to the front of the nave to pin their flowers on the cross, the cross in this church decked out as if for a wedding? In both the church I grew up in and my newly adopted one, the children are front and center. I've heard ministers speak of the dangers of a silent church: it's the baby gurgles and clopping kids' feet and loud whispers and giggles that comfort us that the church moves on, a plant with new shoots. Children remind me of something essential to faith, an easy joy and trust, an openness that shrinks somehow in adulthood.

I think of the paper Christ in my Sunday school class gazing kindly at the children balanced on his two-dimensional knee. I'm thinking about my family and the holiday, and of the man driving my car toward home. This afternoon I'll meet him at a friend's house for Easter dinner. He'll tell me about the show, enormous black and white photographs, and the artist, his friend in the pink cowboy hat, cradling two dozen roses. I will taste his mouth, and will no longer be upset for having been left to worship alone. I'll kiss that sweet spot under his chin and slip a tiny stuffed rabbit, a symbol of who knows what, into his jacket pocket.

• • •

As a child in church, I thought it a rare treat to sit in the balcony, two narrow pews with a bird's-eye view of the congregation below. I sat there during one of the services in a weeklong revival by a preacher brought up from Georgia to rekindle our fire for God. This preacher asked before every service that we bow our heads and close our eyes. If we were willing to let the Spirit move however he would in our hearts, the preacher asked us to raise our hands to signify *yes*. I didn't want the preacher to think I was cold to the workings of God, but I also wasn't ready to say I'd do anything. Rather than raise my hand, I imagined an invisible hand inside of me, and I lifted it in my ribcage, letting God know I did want to be revived, but I was cautious.

One year the high school Sunday school class made a three-dimensional model of the Israelites' tabernacle, like a floor plan with short walls. The high schoolers were too cool to talk to me, but I crept up to the balcony after church one Sunday to look at their model. The tabernacle, splayed out like a social studies fair project, reminded me of a dollhouse. A very spartan dollhouse. Over time I would learn to yearn for the God in others, that the touch of others could be the touch of Christ, a hand held and a word breathed of peace. That afternoon in the balcony I wanted a God I could touch. I wanted to get my hands on his house. I fingered the skinny flap of cloth, a strip of gauze, hanging in the doorway to the holy of holies. I dared touch inside, stroking the wings of the gilded, brittle seraphim.

6

Heal
Me

by Stephanie Tombari

I couldn't have given this faith healing thing a chance a year ago. I wasn't open. God was still on my blacklist for not having the decency to brand me one hundred percent certifiable instead of condemning me to a life of mediocre madness.

Sure, I'd give my right arm to be well, but the image of charismatic evangelical preachers smacking heads and hollering "Be healed!" to a bunch of wide-eyed Jesus seekers writhing in spasms on the altar floor seemed, well, nuts. Those hands a-pumpin' in the churches of the religious right are an unfamiliar sight from the pew I sat in most of my life.

Even folks in the United Church of Canada who were raised to graze in the grassroots are only moderately conservative members of this liberally left denomination. In this two-million-strong, Grand Poobah of Canadian Protestant churches, hands are more commonly raised in protest. Advocacy against the occupation of Palestine and for homosexual rights has found support in the United Church. Nearly all who walk through its doors can expect such a warm, "How do you do?" that some evangelicals—and even a few of the church's own members—have most surely preached the denomination's damnation. Yes, the United Church is where the socially rejected and morally maimed are accepted—the perfect place for a mental case like me.

I don't recall hearing the words "faith healing" when I was growing up in the United Church. But when I did hear them—some time during my university days—my brain formed a visual definition of zombie-like believers thirsting for physical proof that God exists. These were the "evangelicals," and the truth was I had no desire to place my body or my mind in the hands of people I didn't trust.

But there's something to be said for desperation, and living with mental illness is living on the brink. Bipolar II disorder (a.k.a. manic depression, though the term is politically incorrect today) is the mood-shifting, brain-twisting, relationship-annihilating illness I call my own. Until I began taking medication, I had little control over my widely shifting moods. Even still, the monsters pay me a visit now and then. When I flat-line, I want to rip off my skin to escape my body. I wake up through the night drenched in sweat. My only entertainment is conjuring up theatrical ways to end my life.

The other end of the mood spectrum is no pony ride either. In a group therapy session, one woman with depression lamented she wished she had the highs of hypomania (the manic episodes I experience that are not typically characterized by hallucinations and delusions) because the reduced need for sleep and drive that comes with it sounded appealing. Somehow she missed my tears over uncontrollable spending, embarrassing verbal marathons, aggressive behavior, and self-confidence inflated to the point of believing I'm almost invincible.

So as freaky as the idea was, I resolved to give my medication a boost by trying faith healing. With little knowledge on the subject and scarce amounts of nerve to ask around, I did what any inquiring mind would do: I googled it. Link led to link led to a legend among healing churches in North America, right in my own backyard: Toronto Airport Christian Fellowship (TACF).

If you haven't heard of TACF, think giant Southern tent revival meets the United Nations. The diversity in the population—of age, race, and culture—is beautiful. Over a thousand people from more than fifty countries all wanting to worship together suggests to me something good must be going on—that, or something completely Waco (not "wacko"). In January 1994, the church experienced the media-dubbed "Toronto Blessing" once described by TACF as a transferable anointing by the Holy Spirit. Ever since pastors, members, and visitors have experienced "the fire of the Holy Spirit" through uncontrollable laughing, falling to the floor, speaking in tongues, prophesy, and yes, healing. More than three hundred thousand have flocked to experience the fire; I was going to make it one more.

There are a number of choices on the healing menu at TACF. One can attend worship services on Sunday, and hope to be healed in the collective. One can attend any number of free private sessions with a prayer team in the healing room on Tuesdays, between the hours of 10 a.m. and 12 p.m. or 7 p.m. and 8 p.m. Or if you have a week and twelve hundred Canadian dollars (two thousand Canadian dollars for couples), you can attend an intense healing retreat at various times throughout the year. Options one and two, I determined, would be best to satisfy my curiosity and hunger to find out if maybe one day I might be A-okay.

But as I psyched up my mind for healing, the knowledge that some Christians swear mental illness comes from darker forces suppressed my appetite. Dr. Dwight L. Carlson, author of *Why Do Christians Shoot Their Wounded?* (InterVarsity, 1994) coined the term "emotional health gospel," which refers to the belief that mental illness is caused by spiritual issues and character flaws. Therefore, the logic goes, the church can handle treatment and/or healing on its own.

Here's the roll-on-the-floor irony: I once paid good money to ingest similar hooey for a master's degree in biblical counseling. But in my defense, I enrolled shortly after being born again, following a brief hiatus from Christianity. I was ablaze to do good in Jesus' name! It wasn't long before Jesus and I had a heart to heart about my vocational path, and three courses into biblical counseling I dropped the program.

So who subscribes to this "emotional health gospel" idea anyway? Surely not my friends, including the evangelicals in the bunch. Some of their distant cousins it seems, feel strongly otherwise. I can't tell you what a delight it is to read that I just need to have more faith on some Web site in order to be healed of a medical condition.

Yes, there are some yahoos who embarrass the Christian faith by claiming that 270,000 Canadians suffer from bipolar disorder due to flimsy faith. To this I suggest they pray for mental illness so they might gain some perspective. But thinking people of faith, including a United Church minister, a Lutheran pastor, a Christian psychotherapist, and even a prayer team member at TACF, agree mental illness is a medical condition requiring some form of treatment, like cancer or diabetes.

Two days before my first trip to TACF, the church responded to an email I'd sent a month earlier asking if I could be healed. They directed me to Dr. Grant Mullen, who has spoken to their congregation on a few occasions and is an expert in mood disorders. He also happens to be a Christian and the lead medical doctor at the mood disorder clinic I attend for treatment. That said, one of the required readings for participants in a TACF Healing Week is a book by Chester and Betsy Kylstra, called *An Integrated Approach to Biblical Healing Ministry* (Sovereign Word, 2003). The Kylstras are also founders of Restoring the Foundations Ministry. According to their Web site, their ministry helps bring healing to problem areas like generational sin and the resulting curses (which is one explanation I've read for mental illness) and demonic oppression (that too), which sounds frighteningly too much like an emotional health gospel to me. In the case of generational sin, chronic problems like mental illness could be a divine curse as a result of big, fat whopper sins carried out by family in the past. So, sins from one generation can be handed down to the next like family heirlooms, which could manifest in the form of sexual addiction, alcoholism, or yes, even mental illness. Now there is a dowry worth bragging about!

Still, there are some who believe they can interpret several Scripture references to back up their claim: "The Lord is slow to anger, and abounding in steadfast love, forgiving iniquity and transgression, but by no means clearing the guilty, visiting the iniquity of the parents upon the children to the third and the fourth generation" (Numbers 14:18). The trick to healing, then, is praying to God for forgiveness of your family's wanton ways.

A glance back at my own gene pool—three generations on my father's side with bipolar, alcoholism, and depression—earned the concept of generational sin at least some consideration. The idea sounded ridiculous to me, but there's a lot to be said for desperation.

I was prepared to take the sins of my familial past, including my own, to God in the TACF healing room.

Before committing myself to solitary healing, however, I waded around in the general populace at TACF for worship one Sunday in September of 2006. My friend Karen agreed to come along, releasing my Catholic-raised husband from any arm-waving henceforward. It was the quintessential evangelical worship service, tied up like a Christmas package with an altar call at the end.

I could easily carry on about what disturbed me during those two-and-a-half hours, but I'll stick to a few interesting details. Like the little strawberry blonde girl worshipping in the aisle. No more than four years old, she rocked back and forth on her hips with her arms extended wide. Without careful observation, her actions may have been construed as rehearsal for a Stephen King flick. But she wasn't in a trance. She wasn't mimicking. She was genuinely worshipping God, with every ounce of love her tiny body could offer.

But what were those teens up to, in a chorus line across center stage? They'd had an amazing experience at summer camp, the pastor explained. Way out where they had burned campfires, the Holy Spirit descended on them with . . .

"FIRE!" they yelled in unison, stretching their hands to the buzzing crowd. As Mary is holy, I nearly started sniveling in fear as the kids came down the aisles, eager to share their gift with anyone willing to receive. My comfort zone had officially been breached.

Now, had I expected collapsing bodies to seem sane that day, I might have laid off my meds and joined in the holy high jinks of the madhouse. There was the woman gibbering in tongues and jerking her arms high over her head. There was the fifty-something man doing the Harlem shuffle up and down center aisle. And there was the human chain, elbows linked together and flailing about like six-year-olds playing a game of Red Rover.

I might not have gone back for faith healing at all, if the bizarreness of that introductory experience at TACF hadn't given way to something that actually made sense.

John Arnott, founding pastor of TACF, winged a sermon he claimed was motivated by a holy nudge. He said there were people in the audience who needed to hear certain things. These are the only words I remember hearing: "Some think, 'I've been so bad, I don't even think God could forgive me.' Well you're the one he came for. Forgive yourself."

In a room that size, you don't expect to be found. But his words were like a finger pointed directly in my face. At first I was ashamed, but just a few seconds later the mercy in those words registered where the brain makes the face do things like smile. And I remembered the many discussions we'd had about healing in therapy group: Meds are necessary but not always enough. Forgiveness is the one treatment in my ongoing healing I have yet to administer or feel is deserved.

On our way out, I asked Steve Long, a senior pastor at TACF and speaker on healing ministry, what I should do to prepare for the healing room. He smiled, and with a chuckle said four not-so-simple words: "Prepare to be healed."

It took nine days for me to feel prepared. When I showed up alone on a quiet Tuesday, the tension and fear that had lingered after my Sunday visit to TACF faded away. With steady hand, I signed myself in behind six others then watched promo videos about God's love and forgiveness while waiting my turn. An hour-and-a-half later I was greeted by Michael, an older, wise-looking man with snow-white hair. He guided me into a large, windowless room partitioned into small spaces of a less overwhelming size. There I met Lalaima, a short, middle-aged Indian woman with a warm smile. She asked if she could anoint me with oil, then marked my forehead and palms with what smelled like Patchouli in the sign of the cross, the first of many firsts that day for a girl raised in a church where incense was reserved for the Baby Jesus. Rather unexpectedly, she took my hands and held them lightly as Michael placed his hand on top of my head. Then, they started to pray. They prayed for healing of my illness. They prayed I give over my healing to Jesus. They prayed the wall of guilt and shame would fall down. And then, with their hands still laid upon me, they told me to pray out loud.

Under normal circumstances, I couldn't do it. But before they asked again, I whispered a request for healing and forgiveness, for me and all those in my family who had died at the hand of this monster of the mind.

I must have felt safe. There's no other explanation for my vulnerability. Not once was I afraid that these "evangelicals" were doing something sinister or placing bets against me. During the session, Lalaima moved her hands firmly to either side of my head. She later explained that she did it because she felt a leading by the Spirit. The thing was, she didn't have to explain. I felt completely safe in her hands.

When my healing time was over I knew right away I'd experienced something good, but couldn't quite find the right word to describe it. Ten minutes into the ride home it came to me: Clean. Guilt and shame had dissolved like salt in water. "This is a sweet anointing, Stephanie," Michael said while he prayed. I believed him because I had tasted the sweetness too.

The anointing was not so sweet that regular worship in a sea of waving hands at TACF would ever feel sane. But in those healing hands, my burdens felt light and I felt worthy again. Twenty minutes of that feeling, after rarely having it at all, wasn't enough.

"Come back as often as you'd like," Michael said as I was leaving.

"Yes," I answered. And I meant it. I knew that when I sense that day coming, when meds can't stop a rocket ride to mania or a slow boat into the dark, I will call on them for faith healing again.

• • •

So do I feel healed of bipolar disorder? No, not yet. But then again, I guess it depends on what counts as healing. Shortly after I left TACF that day, I had a chat with a friend who works in children's ministry at my church. We talked about miraculous healings we'd heard of and how cool it was that God does stuff like that. But we also talked about the absence of physical healing when what might be needed is a spiritual or emotional revival instead. In my case, a healing of spirit may be more important than a physiological purge of my mental condition. Like I said, having bipolar disorder can really suck. But a dead spirit might do a hell of a lot more damage in the end.

Just before finishing this piece, I heard on a radio show that positive thinking is proven to improve mood. Though this was not earth shattering information, I wrote it down. When you have an illness like bipolar disorder, there can never be enough weapons in your arsenal. Eventually the day comes when you'd do just about anything to be healed, when you no longer care who knows you're not completely right in the head. Those who love me do so despite some of the nightmares bipolar illness brings to their lives. As for my judges, well, the truth is, I prefer to be identified with the mad and misunderstood than those who claim to have it all figured out. It's one reason why I went willingly for healing by people who had once freaked me out. And though we don't go to the same churches, we get our passion from the same Book. And in this upside-down world we all have our part to do—the crazy, the crackpot, and every kook in between.

7

A Hymnal to
Carry

by Andrea Saylor

As a kid I believed hymnals were collectively owned property, safe to steal. Other church items required due process or payment for personal use. Library books you checked out, church facilities rented for a fee, and the church copy machine cost ten cents a copy (unless you made handouts for Sunday school). Leftover crackers and grape juice from Communion were marginally acceptable to take, since I came from a denomination with evangelical and Anabaptist roots that did not view bread as Christ's literal body. But we snuck bites of the flaky Communion crackers guiltily. Hymnals, though, I felt at liberty to carry home with me and keep indefinitely. They were communal and democratic.

Like the voting guides my parents consulted before entering curtained booths on Election Day, hymnals signified democracy because of the rule that Everyone Should Participate. I joined the kids' choir; the directors, in a small room behind the sanctuary, taught us to sing parts. We produced a musical each spring, with angel costumes or cardboard-box time machines that transported us through church music history and let us meet John Wesley and Fanny Crosby. Most kids attended the public school in our middle-class, mostly white, Pennsylvania town, and many of us learned the trumpet or violin. After a few years of lessons, they put us in ensembles during Christmas or Easter services that featured majestic, orchestral songs. As a violinist, I had thrilling moments stumbling through the sixteenth notes of the Hallelujah chorus. The youth handbell choir played several times a year, its white-gloved row accompanying the collection plates' passages. Each Sunday morning some assortment of these singers and musicians performed songs they'd practiced the Wednesday night before.

Of course, we did not usually consider church music *performance.* Along with lessons in pronunciation, while singing we imbibed spiritual and moral direction that demonstrated a dichotomy between music as entertainment and music as worship. Sometimes the two blended, as when our Southern-bred pastor brought out his banjo during Saturday night gatherings or when the reformed flower child played her solo songs that sounded like Joni Mitchell softly praising Jesus. Also, we became temporary stars in our children's musicals. At the age of six my younger brother held an inflatable guitar and pretended to rock out, then rode a stick pony while wearing a plastic knight's helmet, to the backdrop of the rest of us kids wearing angel's wings and singing a song to narrate his actions. I forget the song's spiritual point; I remember his performance and how popular it was.

These shows were good clean fun, accepted by the church. But even the goofy moments had meaning. I know that whatever words we sang behind my brother's antics illustrated some lesson. And, to make matters more complex, most church music, especially on Sunday mornings, aimed not merely to illuminate spiritual wisdom or reinforce moral codes, but to promote actual interaction with God. These acts of praise or worship, therefore, we directed to God, and they were not meant to earn applause or foster a sense of pride in our musical abilities. We did not perform for the congregation, which we did not call an audience. Rather, we guided them into worship both musically and, through the lyrics, spiritually. Congregants usually sang along with whoever was on stage (an area of the sanctuary we referred to vaguely as "up front" since "stage" sounded crass and entertainment-minded). So I learned that everyone takes part in music designed to speak to the object and inspiration and creator of that music—God.

Because we directed our music to God, we only used unabashedly religious words like "praise," "worship," or even "glorify," to describe the thing we attempted on Sunday mornings. In a strange way, this empowered us. Not only *could* we sing, we were *expected* to. Mostly, the congregation sang along with the choirs. Sure, sometimes the little kids' choir sang a song all by themselves or the adult choir sang a difficult arrangement—not infrequently something I found corny—they had prepared. But unless you ran the sound system, played an instrument, or were physically unable, you sang. In our musicals, almost everybody had a solo, regardless of talent. Mine was a two-liner from the hymn "Fairest Lord Jesus." I sang it when I was about ten and hoped people thought my voice sounded sweet. We learned to sing church songs well when we were in choir, and when we weren't, we sang them well from the pews. Just as church music meant downplaying the idea of performance, it also meant blurring the boundaries between audience and performer.

It didn't occur to me until years later that some people do not grow up singing together regularly. Some people are never told that they, too, can and should sing, and that singing together is not embarrassing or childish but important, both emotionally and spiritually. I learned that you sing together. My mother advised me that taking our key tool, the hymnal, to our house was fine, and I did. I practiced the hymns for Sunday service on my violin or bass guitar. Sometimes I just looked at them and read the lyrics that I liked. Some we sang often; I may have memorized their melodies and refrains before I could read.

We sang plenty of songs that weren't hymns, too. Listening to grown-ups talk and reading Christian magazines, I knew that outside our church, in much of evangelical America, great debates and church splits occurred over the very divisive subject of church music. I never heard much of this debate at our church, which didn't act as though "traditional" and "contemporary" music were mutually exclusive. Sometimes we played hymns with guitars and drums or with organs. Sometimes we sang contemporary praise choruses. Sometimes, thanks to visiting missionaries or the ethnomusicologist who was our church's music director, we sang in Spanish or Swahili. Like the melting-pot image of American democracy, at church, you can sing all styles of music as long as you sing them with real worship in your heart.

As a teenager, I still loved most of the music, but the worship part started to become confusing. I didn't know how to tell if we really worshipped or just sang. Sometimes I felt great emotion, but sometimes I didn't. Sometimes I didn't really think about God at all. Music was so physical and so immediate, so visceral—even in my central Pennsylvania town where folks looked awkward just clapping. What if some of us did music for its own sake and not for God? Emotions tricked you; I learned this by watching my peers' messy romances and by noticing our tendency to live two-faced lives, according to fluctuating ethics. If you could praise God on Sunday, and then sin on Monday, maybe you sang for the same reason you sinned: it felt good. And feeling good during worship was acceptable, even desired, but how could you tell if the good feelings came from God? It seemed like worship required the mental, emotional, and physical gymnastics of thinking about God being great, feeling God being great, and singing on key at once.

But I decided that, since God liked music, making our thoughts theologically sound while we sang probably didn't matter completely. I also learned that God's number one trait was love and therefore forgiveness. And that meant God would forgive us for sometimes enjoying the melody more than we enjoyed worshipping him. So, when at fourteen I learned to play bass guitar, I contented myself knowing that while I focused on my fingers and the strings and the deep, satisfactory sound from my amp, most of the congregants focused on praising and glorifying God in their worship. As a church musician, even if I was a little confused or lacked adequate emotional fervor about Jesus, I helped the people around me worship—and that was enough.

• • •

All of this experience underwent great testing and reconsideration in college. First, I had to decide where, whether, and how to go to church, which I had never considered a conscious decision. My Christian liberal arts college did not require church attendance but bombarded freshman with church options: emails, fliers, bulletin boards, and word-of-mouth invitations advertised local churches, and they often provided a van shuttle for car-less students. Many of us church-hopped aggressively. We attended sporadically and usually with little involvement beyond Sunday mornings. We also went to different churches depending on our mood or our friends. At my church at home, everyone knew my name and my parents. In college, I blended into rotating groups of fickle college attendees; somebody we didn't know greeted us with a warm handshake and gave us pale blue fliers about young adult Bible studies and social functions, which we rarely attended.

I can think of at least four churches I attended multiple times in succession. At these churches, I discovered traditional liturgical worship for the first time. Infatuation followed my initial meeting. I loved the formality and reverence of the words, and I loved the faithfulness I felt in repetition, which allowed me to think that I could still worship even if I did not feel emotional about God. Most of all, I loved taking the Eucharist, which, up until my sophomore year of college, I had always referred to as "Communion." At home, it consisted of grape juice and crackers passed to us on a plate. Here, the capital-E Eucharist was wine and bread and you had to walk to the front of the room to get it from the priest, and it was the climax of the service every single week.

A British pastor in a Lutheran church in a small town initiated me into this tradition. My Bible-major roommate knew him from school, and we sat in his office where he passionately explained why taking the Eucharist each week fulfilled something in the human heart that trite, contemporary evangelical services, with their careless, occasional "Communion" and trendy music could not. (That was his tone, if not his exact phrasing.) We took his words with a grain of salt; by then I believed in a God who worked with lots of styles and traditions and in nature as well as in church walls. But I partly agreed. I wanted accountability and something big and somber enough to respond to all my questions about God. Effusive songs about feeling good felt cheap and false.

Another semester I attended an Episcopal church in the inner city. Half of the small, elderly, African-American congregation comprised the choir, who wore robes of black, green, orange, and yellow and sang old spirituals and gospel songs half a beat ahead of the pianist. The services lasted an eternity and the priest felt comfortable dispensing his political views along with his gospel readings in his rambling sermons. Where the liturgy read "God of Abraham, Isaac, and Jacob," he said, "God of Abraham and Sarah, Isaac and Rebecca, Jacob and Rachel." I loved this more than the Lutheran church.

But I never got into the music. I appreciated that the simple and not-so-tuneful Lutheran songs complimented the strain of speaking archaically and that the old gospel tunes at the Episcopal church came from a rich history I barely knew. But the music didn't grip me or make me want to keep singing. I never felt chords tingling in my feet.

Still, I preferred these to contemporary songs. I felt a growing disdain for many of the praise choruses I was raised singing and much more disdain for the new ones I heard at school, where we had to attend morning chapel twice a week. The questions I felt as a teenager playing my bass no longer sat quietly under contentment with the music. They roared at me when I sang. I didn't feel okay saying that I simply didn't feel as excited about Jesus as everybody else did. I had to wonder if it was really Jesus everybody liked, or just the sense of meaning they found in a God they made up and the emotional intimacy they fabricated while singing. How could you know this stuff was true? How could communities who sang praises every week to the God of love continue the back-stabbing, apathy, prejudice, and materialism my college classes and experiences showed ran rampant in American culture? What good was religion if the world fell to pieces as we continued to sing? Normal questions for any Christian or college student, but feeling them for the first time hurt like hell. And a lot of my friends felt the same way.

My friend Haley came to my dorm room one day with a mix CD of a band called Over the Rhine, whose music she proselytized to me heavily. As a girl, she had attended an informal house church because her parents found institutional and ritualized religion empty and disturbing. She wrote something on a three-by-five note card and stuck it between a stack CD cases next to my desk. She went back to her homework. Later I picked up the note card and saw one line of lyric from a song on her CD: "I'm not letting go of God, I'm just losing my grip." Capriciously, like God, she left the note without explanation. It could have meant "I like this song," or it could have summarized what we felt about life, religion, and relationships. Like God, and hymns, I remembered it.

In the midst of our questions and tensions, contemporary worship seemed like brainless, emotionally driven theology set to bad pop music. For instance, the popular song "I Could Sing of Your Love Forever" made me want to take a fork to my ears. Over one, maybe two chords of repetitive guitar or keyboard, the lyrics consist mostly of that single line sung repeatedly, for however long the worship leader feels like singing. Democratically, I believed Christians had the right to sing such songs as genuine expressions of faith. But like Hollywood romances, the unoriginal music floated, blithely, outside of my reality. I *couldn't* sing of God's love forever, and, considering all the problems in the world and how troubling faith seemed to me, I didn't think I should.

I was scared. I saw other Christians feel good vibrations while singing love songs to Jesus, the same songs that just made me feel distant. I really hoped that didn't mean I was distant from Jesus. But I had so many questions about my faith and had changed my opinion about enough significant topics that I thought maybe I had to be. I wasn't letting go of God; I was just losing my grip.

As I discovered that Christian pop songs, books, and other vestiges of faith could turn on me, become suspect, and lose their meaning, one churchy object never let me dismiss it: the confiscated hymnal that sat on my dorm-room shelf. My favorite, most familiar hymns remained capable of convincing me of the gravity and reality of their content. They were musically simple but rich because of their harmonies. The words were at least complicated enough to give me something to think about. Unlike the liturgical tunes, I knew them well and could dig into them instead of limping through an unknown melody with other timid parishioners. Unlike the contemporary songs, they never felt too blithely happy.

I could not dismiss melodies and harmonies that had lived for generations or their reverent, faithful tones. As my grown-up questions made faith feel less certain, hymns still felt like rocks and anchors, biblical metaphors for steadfast things. Their melodies stayed etched in my brain and didn't let me go. As always, I questioned if

God or the music itself persisted. And as I always had, I decided that I could not separate the two easily and that this imprecision was not wrong.

• • •

This year, one-and-a-half years after graduating college, I returned to my hometown church for a Christmas Eve service. I knew all the hymns' harmonies by heart, having played them on the violin for years. The congregation that I grew up with surprised me with their voices, which I had not heard for over a year. Their voices swelled, nearly eclipsing the piano. They sounded round and full; they vibrated the pews, hymnals, lungs, and rafters. Their voices went down to my feet. Their words were strong and clear. They were not swallowed by guitars or uncertainty. They were not timid or awkward, following foreign notes led by choirs who did not need them. There was no center or stage. Couples and families peered into shared hymnals, their mouths forming reverent Os:

> Come, thou long-expected Jesus, born to set thy people free.
> From our fears and sins release us; let us find our rest in thee.

Like a bellows, the sanctuary breathed in and out unrealized hopes and honest belief. The people knew what to sing, and everyone took part. They sang the melodies and harmonies they had sung every year before that and would sing every year after. I thought of how I used to mystify Haley: my love for hymns in the midst of shifting ideas and faith crises baffled her. But when one of our professor's wives died, she wrote me a letter about the funeral, where old hymns and folks who knew how to sing them surrounded her. "Sweetie," she wrote, "from those few moments alone, I understand you now more than ever; why you think the way you do about hymns, and why you can *sing*."

8

Exorcizing the

Spirit

by Anastasia McAteer

During my years at an evangelical college, which shall remain nameless, I sojourned among the theater folk. We would go on retreat every year, and as arty Christian people do, we'd close the day with a worship service that was spontaneous and free, involving a lot of candles and people piping up in prayer or song, with others joining in or sitting quietly. The retreat was a highlight of my freshman year. But sophomore year, something very strange happened.

We got to the time in the service when people could lift up prayers, poems, songs, or other offerings, and it was going along quite nicely. We heard some Scripture passages and sang a few songs (I did *not* repeat my freshman mistake of trying to get everyone to sing "Lord I Lift Your Name On High"—they must have hated me!). I began to sense my spirit lifting, and happily anticipated the coming "God high."

All of a sudden I heard what sounded like screams, very far off. At first we kept singing, trying to ignore the noise. But the shrieks got louder and more insistent. We then heard other voices, jumbled shouts, growing ever closer. I opened my eyes and peeked around, noticing others doing the same.

A few moments later, the doors to the chapel burst open and a bewildering commotion entered. Several of my peers were running up the center aisle carrying one of the girls from the group above their heads. She was the person screaming. Her eyes rolled, large and

69

wild, and her arms thrashed about. Her white knuckles punched the air as she twisted and contorted. And she made the most horrible sounds. This was a girl I knew. A Christian girl. An actor, too, as were most of us in the room.

They threw her down on the altar. She flailed all around, fighting as they tried to hold her down. Those around her responded to her every move by yelling at whatever they thought was causing it, screaming rebukes at the empty air. Suddenly she stared at a specific location ahead of her and pointed, spewing gibberish. At this, those around her began verbally attacking whatever it was she was supposedly looking at. My professor, our group leader, jumped into the fray—we waited, breathless, for him to save us—but instead he began *speaking in tongues!*

They were trying to exorcize something from her. This was not in the college brochure.

I'd never seen anything like this before. But I'd heard about it, and I'd been raised to believe it was dangerous. I was surrounded by a cacophony of frightening noise and people leaping into the air. I half expected Satan himself to manifest at any moment. This young woman said she could see something dark and evil standing before her . . . steps from my seat.

I cowered under the pew. I was choked with terror. A strong sense of evil had filled the room upon their entry, and everything had been thrown into chaos. People were screaming, jumping over pews and acting completely crazy. It was total pandemonium. I slipped out (stepping over bodies along the way) and ran downstairs. There I found a group of my friends—fear in their eyes, shaking—trying to process the experience. We talked about our mutual sense of dread and our doubts about the authenticity of what was going on. I remember quite clearly people saying, "God is a God of order, not of chaos," a quotation from 1 Corinthians. We tried to pray, then sit quietly, waiting for it to pass.

Suddenly the power went out—the electricity, not the Holy Ghost—and the room went black. Everyone screamed. When the fire alarms went off, that was about the maximum any of us could handle, and adrenaline got me outside somehow. Instead of the usual passing of the peace and warm tidings as we took our leave, people departed in opposing groups. Those of us who'd been downstairs didn't make eye contact with those who'd been participating in the "exorcism." We were angry with them for ruining our special service. We felt betrayed and confused by our professor. But we could see people who were still jumping around, now for joy. They seemed to feel wonderful about what had happened. I couldn't bear to talk to them; I left as fast as I could.

I had a lot of tough conversations with my friends that week. Most of the people with whom I was close were equally troubled by what had happened. We felt sure that some kind of explanation would surface that the woman just had a bad breakdown or something. I heard that she'd had previous mental and emotional problems, and she had a reputation as an attention seeker. She had told me long desperate stories of situations involving her danger, which later turned out to be exaggerated. Sadly, what became obvious as I pondered the event was that she was desperately crying out for the attention that had been focused on God to be moved in her direction instead.

Later that week we received a letter from our professor stating that the Holy Spirit had moved powerfully at the service, and it was a gift from God. He added that he'd heard some of us had not been able to "receive" this Spirit-filled worship and needed counseling.

Huh? Apparently those of us who were disturbed by the drama were the ones with mental issues. Otherwise we certainly would have recognized the Spirit at work! We attended a very uncomfortable meeting at which we were essentially ostracized. Our leader made it clear that he believed the Holy Spirit had worked through the "exorcists," and anyone who didn't feel uplifted by the experience—or who questioned its authenticity—was out of sync not only with the group but with God. I was sad and confused, feeling like I'd missed out on something important; I was also ashamed for thinking it was fake. I left the theater group for the rest of that leader's tenure, even though he was a man I greatly respected and admired.

I also decided that if *that* was God's spirit at work, I wanted nothing to do with it. I hated the chaos and the fear that came along with it. I hated that only a few had the privelege of being included, while the rest of us just had to take it on faith that it was good and holy. I had grown up being taught that charismatics weren't good

Christians because they were overly emotional and dabbled in dangerous spiritual forces. As a teenager, I'd been forbidden to go on a street-drama missions trip with a large, internationally recognized parachurch organization, for the simple reason that they stated in their materials that they would not hinder any manifestations of the Spirit, including speaking in tongues. That was enough for my church to deny my support and my participation. The experience at the "exorcism" reinforced these fears.

The Holy Spirit had always been something of a nebulous concept for me, anyway. My church of origin, a midwestern Evangelical Free Church, taught that the charismatic gifts in the New Testament existed for that time only and did not continue past the apostolic era. The Spirit had done a lot of amazing things for the disciples in the early church, but I got the sense that he hadn't been around before Jesus and really didn't do much after the church got going. The few glimpses of Christian history that I gained from Sunday school made me think that the Spirit went on a break from about AD 100 until the Reformation—or really, until our denomination's founding a couple hundred years ago (not to say everyone at our church believed this, but such were my childhood impressions). Now the Spirit's work was to help us to read and understand God's Word, and that was about it.

For years after college, any time someone would do anything remotely charismatic (even just lifting a hand during worship), my stomach would tie up in knots, as I waited to hear the screams from the back of the sanctuary. I couldn't face the possibility of such terror, so I would simply exit the situation. Nowadays it's quite common in most evangelical churches for people to lift their hands in worship, especially when a song instructs them to do so. But when I was growing up, hand-raising was considered part of a larger superstitious theological system that also sought "manifestations" such as speaking in tongues, faith healing, and even exorcism. Churches like mine wished to move beyond such emotional outbursts into a more reasoned style of worship, focusing on the Word of God preached in song and sermon.

Eventually this meant I couldn't feel comfortable in most evangelical churches. I had been raised in a church that only sang hymns, but when I moved to California, I found the praise chorus revolution was already a few decades old and quite entrenched. Part of singing along to a rock band in church is . . . well . . . rocking out. It means people will dance around and wave their arms just like they do at a rock concert. For me, with my conservative Midwest upbringing, the California praise-and-worship style of church, which grew out of the hippie Jesus Movement of the seventies, among other influences, was a shock to the system. This music sounded relatively current, they used guitars and drums instead of organs, and the people worshipped by moving their bodies. It was a new world for me, a true culture shift.

I found a church with preaching that I loved enough to stand the rocking out, but I remained uncomfortable. As the years passed, I began to realize that there was something deeper that was disturbing me. I wondered whether the people swaying around me had any idea what they were doing or what they were singing about. With eyes closed and hands raised they trilled along to simple melodies with simpler lyrics, heavy on long Al-le-luuuuuuuu-ias. I had to wonder whether this could be called worship. It came to be less frightening, but it didn't seem very, well . . . dignified.

I would try to imagine what was going on in the heads of those around me (if anything). They would stand stiff as a board when we sang the requisite hymn of the morning, but as soon as those guitars and drums kicked in, it was like being at a concert. Or rather, a bad imitation of a concert. Visiting more evangelical churches through the years, I found that many churches eventually gave up altogether on hymns and other "boring" liturgical elements like Scripture readings or responsive congregational prayer, preferring instead that the breaks between songs be filled with improvisation: "We just wanna thank you, Father God, for this morning, and we just come before you now, and we just wanna feel your presence," et cetera, ad nauseam. I began to wonder why we were all wasting our time at church when we could see a better show in the club on Saturday night (without the weird ad-libbing). Seriously, you wouldn't be able to tell the difference, at least from the audience reaction. People would comment after worship that it was a really great experience, and what they usually meant was that they'd had a spiritual or emotional high during the music. They would use the same language one would use about an arena show or a pep rally. Was this really all that there was when it came to worshipping an infinite God? After rocking out for four years, I decided I needed church to be completely different from everything else I did in my life. Why bother attending, otherwise?

As I realized evangelical worship, as I'd experienced it, was not going to work for me, I began to understand that the seeds for these feelings had been planted during that fateful night in college. Worship as primarily designed for an individual "experience" just seemed wrong. I had seen how bad things can get when each person has his or her own definition of the Spirit's "gifts" and there is no consensus on what is and is not of God. I began to long for worship that wasn't about me or my feelings—that was somehow objectively real, vital, connected to others and to God. I wished I could encounter God in a way that was communal, that couldn't be accidentally missed by anyone in the room, and couldn't leave anyone out. But I had no idea how to find this.

I left the evangelical church. On Sunday mornings, I went to the beach instead. Floating in the water, I felt part of something larger than myself. I began to wonder if I'd ever bother with church again. The ocean was so powerful yet so comfortable for me. It was how I wanted God to be.

But it was hard for me to be out of community with other Christians. I didn't like evangelical worship and theology because it was so individualistic, but I had fallen into the same pattern of being a spiritual loner. I knew I couldn't sustain any kind of relationship with God on my own, especially because I didn't feel I could trust the Holy Spirit. I'm a church-goer at heart, and I could only stay away for a couple of weeks.

Yet I couldn't go back to any place where God was supposed to be my buddy. The ocean taught me that God was way bigger than I could imagine. Somewhere along the line, I learned the meaning of the word transcendence, and I hungered for it. I wanted mystery. And history. And community.

I eventually found an Episcopal church, and my first weeks there were like coming home. For several Sundays, I wept through the entire service. I didn't really understand why I was so emotional, especially at the Eucharistic prayers. I just knew that all of a sudden God was bigger than I'd ever imagined yet also somehow closer. God was my friend on some level, but also dangerous. The fears I'd felt before were not erased but were put in their proper context along-side a God who could be trusted.

And I learned that the Holy Spirit has been up to an awful lot in the last two thousand years. I learned about her presence in the sacraments, about her presence in the body of Christ—a mystical connection between people worshipping in my church. I learned to call the Spirit "she," for many reasons, but most importantly because I'd learned to love the feminine qualities in God. It may sound ridiculously rosy, but it was home, and my spirit just *settled* there. Of course, I've been there long enough now to discover what Episcopalians don't do so well, and what kinds of worship varia-tions within our denomination are bothersome to me. But overall, I found that the *Book of Common Prayer* (our worship manual) rests on centuries-old tradition that has mostly figured out how best to access God—through much trial and error, to be sure. Newer ex-periments can be risky propositions that are likely to fail. I, for one, found that I was tired of being a lab rat.

I had to leave the evangelical church because I had to find a connection to Christianity that went back to the beginning, even us-ing liturgies that can be traced nearly that far. To find a God I could trust, I had to find God in the community of love around me, not in my own decision or beliefs. I could trust the church that had writ-ten the creeds, that had formed rhythms of prayer, that had spent hundreds of years in worship together, feeding on Christ's body and blood, baptizing the new into the faith, and laying the dead in God's arms. Even when I am afraid or confused or questioning, I know that I am not alone: neither in my doubts, nor in the answers that I will find. I know that the Spirit is guiding the church (slowly and mysteriously) toward the fulfillment of God's agenda for the earth. I've joined the rushing river of her kingdom work, and I am happy to be carried along.

Most wonderfully, this has healed my very old, deep wounds. For I am now able to raise my hands with the rest of my church on the best day of the year: Easter. It is the only day we offer this gesture at our particular parish, underlining the centrality and spirit of the celebration. It isn't taken for granted, it isn't forced, and it grows organically from a rush of the Spirit that lifts our hands and hearts to God as we proclaim the risen Lord. At that moment, we are not individuals; we are a symphony of sound and a mass of humanity that is lifted up as one. I am safe in my place among the members of Christ's body, and I can stay there forever.

Train Up a Child
in the Way
She Should Go

EDUCATION

9

Quick and
Powerful

by Hannah Faith Notess

At the height of my devotion to daily Bible reading, when I was about sixteen, I could be found each morning before school curled in the big yellow chair next to my bed. I'd sit tucked up in a blanket with my Bible in my lap and all my supplies around me. I had a highlighter for important verses, my journal and pen in case the passage inspired further reflection, and my "Read the Bible in a Year" pamphlet, with its neat row of boxes to check off, one for every day. I had everything I needed.

The one piece of this picture of piety that didn't quite fit?

Half the time I was fast asleep.

• • •

I started in on the Bible pretty early. When my mom realized I was old enough to hear a TV commercial at a friend's house once and parrot it exactly (we didn't have a TV), she figured I might as well put my verbal abilities to good use. So I began at age four with the usual suspects: the short verses used to lead somebody to Christ: "All have sinned and fall short of the glory of God" (Romans 3:23), and "For the wages of sin is death, but the free gift of God is eternal life in Christ Jesus our Lord" (Romans 6:23).

Every night after dinner, we'd sit in the living room of the apartment, and my dad would read us—my mom, me, and my two-year-old brother, Brian—a story from the Bible. Then he'd read a chapter from another book, maybe one of the Chronicles of Narnia or a story from *Tales of Old Russia*. Then Brian would be put to bed, and I'd get to stay up a little later and practice my Bible verses.

After the salvation verses, we moved on to the classics—John 3:16, the Lord's Prayer, selections from the twenty-third Psalm. I gulped up the Bible by teaspoonfuls, just the way I picked up "I'm Cuckoo for Cocoa Puffs," or "Silly Rabbit, Trix are for Kids." (My mom refused my pleas concerning these cereals.)

My dad kept a list of the verse references on a half-sheet of paper stuck in his copy of the NASB—the New American Standard Bible, still his translation of choice. The NASB translation remains as close as possible to the original Greek and Hebrew, while getting rid of King James "begats" and "smiting." The publishers have since updated the NASB, but in the eighties, it still addressed God as "Thou." Even the updated version refers to people as "men" and a human being as a "man." Nevertheless, my dad likes the NASB for its plain-Jane approach to translation: nothing extra, just the Word.

Likewise, when he played guitar for our church small group, his favorites were the "Scripture songs." As their name suggested, Scripture songs took only the actual words of the Bible and set them to 1970s folk music. By any standard, Scripture songs are not a new approach to Christian worship; the Psalms were written to be sung, and they contain Hebrew musical notations so ancient even scholars don't know what they mean: "*Selah*" or "To the tune of *Do Not Destroy.*" But what was new about Scripture songs, at least to my parents, was their approachability. One of my mom and dad's friends even wrote Scripture songs herself, recorded them on tapes at home and passed them around, a kind of self-publishing outfit. "The word of God is quick and powerful, sharper than any two-edged sword," was how one of the jauntiest started off.

You could think of Scripture songs as forerunners to the hyped-up, PowerPointed, emotional, praise-band, rock anthems with vaguely biblical-sounding lyrics so popular in megachurches today. But while Scripture songs did use contemporary-sounding music and rhythms, I think they were after a different goal. Their Bible-only lyrics reflected a desire for a pure, simple spirituality that hoped to avoid false emotion, needless ritual. They expressed one of the central longings of evangelicalism—the desire to get closer to that first New Testament church, to go back in time to get closer to Jesus. And, of course, the songs worked as effective mnemonics for memorizing Bible verses. I'm surprised at how many I still know by heart.

Once I had the twenty-third Psalm down, my dad struggled to find verses that would be good for me to memorize. I got the first verse of the Bible—"In the beginning God created the heavens and the earth" (Genesis 1:1)—as well as a few inspirational parts of the prophets: "For surely I know the plans I have for you, says the Lord, plans for your welfare and not for harm, to give you a future with hope" (Jeremiah 29:11).

I cracked, eventually. I must have been about six. The list on the half-sheet of paper had spilled onto a second sheet filled with my dad's small, careful handwriting. It was getting a bit long, and when, as I remember it, one of our nightly sessions brought me to tears of frustration, my parents put the little half-sheet of paper away. Tears wouldn't make for a healthy relationship with the Bible later on, and for now, I'd hit the limit for the amount of Bible I could absorb. We continued to memorize verses, but together, as a family—verses Brian and I could both work on. No more drill sessions.

But I was hardly done with the Bible. A song we sang in Sunday school explained why the Bible was so important:

Read your Bible, pray every day, pray every day, pray every day;
Read your Bible, pray every day, and you'll grow, grow, grow.
Don't read your Bible, forget to pray, forget to pray, forget to pray;
Don't read your Bible, forget to pray, and you'll shrink, shrink, shrink.

The motions that went along with this song required us to crouch down at the beginning, sprout up in the middle with our arms held high like sunflower leaves, and finally, to shrivel and collapse at the end. I can't say I pondered the warning about shrink, shrink, shrinking. I just assumed that, as I grew physically, I'd grow spiritually, in the manner prescribed by the song. My dad sat at his desk early every morning and read his Bible, a chapter or two a day, straight through. When he got to Revelation, he'd start again in Genesis, a practice he continues to this day. I assumed I'd grow up to do the same.

• • •

I got back into memorization when, in third grade, a neighborhood friend invited me to the AWANA program at one of the larger
churches in town. AWANA stands for "Approved Workmen Are Not
Ashamed," a quotation adapted from the King James of 2 Timothy:
"Study to shew thyself approved unto God, a workman that needeth
not to be ashamed, rightly dividing the word of truth." But the structure of AWANA borrowed more from the Boy and Girl Scouts than
from the epistles of the apostle Paul.

Each club meeting began with games. These usually consisted
of standing on the edges of a square—each team along one edge
of the square. Then you were given a number. When your number
was called, you had to rush into the center of the square and grab
something—a rope, a colored bowling pin, a beanbag. Someone always got trampled. Sometimes the trampled kid was me. I hated the
games. I was slow, and I had just gotten glasses, which were always
getting bumped.

After games we split into groups by gender and grade level
for "Handbook Time." Our group, third- and fourth-grade girls, was
called "Chums." During this time, you recited, from your official
AWANA handbook, King James Bible verses to a parent volunteer. Or,
if you hadn't bothered to memorize any, you could just run around
screaming. The mother to whom I recited my verses had two daughters in my age bracket. They were always running around screaming,
and she never made them sit down and recite the King James.

One of the things AWANA had in common with scouting pro-
grams was its seemingly random Native American trappings. On
the back of my Chums blouse was a picture of a slender Indian girl,
leaning into the wind, eyes half-closed, in front of her teepee. A yellow feather jutted from her cheerful blue headband. What did this
girl have to do with being a Chum? In Girl Scouts, I knew, girls got
patches and pins for practical, Indian-like survival skills (tying knots,
camping, baking). We got patches and pins for memorizing Bible
verses, for bringing non-Christian friends to AWANA. How did the
Indian girl fit into this? What did she know about the prophet Isaiah
or about bringing unchurched friends to church? Was I supposed to

evangelize *her*? Could I get a uniform like her supple deerskin dress instead of this boxy gray shirt? If it was hot, you sweated through the uniform, and if it was cold, you had to wear a sweatshirt underneath, which looked even more dorky, if that was possible.

Given my earlier practice, I did okay at saying verses, earning numerous little gold feathers. Still, I loathed every inch of the uniform's tacky polyester. You could earn points by wearing it to school, and I had come to feel a sense of Christian duty regarding my uniform. The Bible said we Christians would have to suffer for our faith. So I wore it to school, suffering an itchy neckline and sweaty armpits for Jesus. But I would not burden my fledgling friendships at school by inviting other girls to become Chums. I would suffer alone.

The Word of God, as my parents' friend had sung, was quick and powerful, sharper than any two-edged sword. I hadn't yet learned that "quick" meant "living," but the verse still made sense to me. Some kind of swift knife, hacking downward from heaven, had cut me off from fitting in at school. The Word of God had pared me neatly away from the other kids as cleanly as my mom peeled the skin off a chicken breast.

Girl Scout uniform day was the same day as AWANA uniform day, and I gazed with envy on the Girl Scouts' green sashes of belonging. I didn't really want to join them. They were kind of snooty. But still, I didn't want the Bible to make me different. There were at least ten girls in kelly green to my one gray blouse. And unlike AWANA, which only offered God's Plan of Salvation, the Girl Scouts were selling something that people actually wanted: cookies.

• • •

The climax of the AWANA year was the AWANA Grand Prix. The leaders handed out a plastic bag containing a block of pinewood, four plastic wheels, and a page of regulations to each child. From these materials, we were to make pinewood derby cars to race down a ramp. I asked my dad to help me saw the block into a car shape and drill holes for the wheel axles. He helped me pick out a paint color from the leftover cans of house paint in the garage. I chose the powder blue of my bedroom walls. We didn't have any black paint, so I colored in the windshield and windows with a permanent marker.

What neither my dad nor I knew, though, was that the Grand Prix's real competition was among fathers. It was a chance for our church's office-job dads to prove to their wives they had a reason to keep all those tools in the garage. They took their sons' (mostly sons) pinewood blocks out of their hands the moment they arrived home with them. They polished the axles and sanded the wheels smooth. They drilled weights into the bottom of the cars, just within the regulation weight limit. They carved the cars into elaborate shapes: a school bus, a Pepsi truck, a banana. They painted the cars with the glossy model airplane paint. My dad approved of the Bible side of AWANA, but he had no more interest in this ritualized display of male ego than I did. We admired our handiwork naively, and he dropped me off—car in hand, Chums blouse buttoned up—at the church for the Grand Prix.

The Grand Prix began with the AWANA theme song. We stood up to sing it, a militaristic anthem that ended with a yell, "Youth on the march," our fists punching the air. The AWANA program's current incarnation may have dropped the Native American paraphernalia, renamed the Chums group "Truth and Training," and replaced the boxy gray uniform with colorful polo shirts with an embroidered logo, but they've kept the militaristic theme song: "Hail, AWANA! On the march for youth! Hail, AWANA! Holding forth the truth!"

The war language didn't bother me back then. We'd memorized Ephesians, which told us that we were to "put on the full armor of God," and that "our struggle is not against flesh and blood." But now, with our country in the throes of a flesh-and-blood war, the memory of a roomful of children in uniform chanting "Youth on the march" freaks me out a little.

After the theme song, we gathered around the special race ramp. Once the cars had been checked out by an AWANA official to ensure they were within the weight limit and hadn't used any illegal materials, the cars raced down the ramp, three at a time. When I saw the first set of shiny cars speed down the ramp and heard the boys whoop and yell, my heart fell. I wanted to remove my car from the race, so I wouldn't be shamed by its homely coat of house paint. But it was too late. It had already been weighed and measured. When its turn came, it floated like a feather down the ramp, finishing what seemed like hours after its two zippy rivals. I stood far from the ramp, pretending like the car wasn't mine. I was glad my dad wasn't there to see us fail. I was dressed like everybody else in a gray uniform, but I felt just as out of place as I did on the public school playground.

AWANA was an attempt by well-meaning adults to break the unwieldy Bible into bite-sized chunks for kids, the way your mother cuts up a steak for you when you're still missing your two front teeth. But all the games, prizes, and trophies just made me feel weird and uncomfortable. Plain old memorizing was the only AWANA task I was any good at.

After two years in AWANA, my parents graciously let me to quit. I'd earned an award for memorization, a wood-veneer plaque with "AWANA" engraved on it. It sat on my bookshelf gathering dust until I finally threw it away.

From then on, the only serious memorizing I did would be each year at summer camp, where you could work toward earning patches (once again, emblazoned with Native Americans) by reciting verses and making crafts. Summer camp was less competitive than AWANA and way more fun—swimming, hikes, crafts, and tons of other activities AWANA couldn't offer. As a teenager, I'd work there four summers in a row as a counselor, listening to my campers recite Bible verses so they could earn their own patches.

• • •

About the time I started as a camp counselor, I started the daily Bible reading thing. We had a camp-wide quiet time every day, a peaceful fifteen-minute period of silence. I'd sit with my back against a big Ponderosa pine, Bible in lap, inhaling the pines' warm butterscotch smell and feeling close to God. I wanted to keep that feeling during the school year. At fifteen I'd received a grown-up Bible for Christmas—New International Version, leather-bound in navy—to replace the kid's Bible I'd lugged around till then. And on the last Sunday of each year, a daily Bible reading plan for the next year came tucked into the church bulletin. Next to each day of the year, two Bible passages, one Old Testament and one New Testament, were listed with a little box to check once you'd completed the reading. I thought I'd start with the New Testament and save the messy Old Testament for later. So beginning in the middle of my sophomore year of high school, I read through the entire New Testament. Every time I came to a verse that sounded familiar, I highlighted it. By the end of the year, the books of the New Testament, especially Paul's letters, were pretty well colored in.

The next year, I repeated the New Testament. But then a funny thing started to happen. Every morning before school, I'd curl up in the chair beside my bed and open my Bible on my lap. But as soon as I stared at the page, my eyes would go all blurry. I couldn't manage to turn the letters on the page into words that meant anything.

Then the sleeping started.

I'd doze off right in the middle of chapters; one minute Jesus would be healing lepers, and the next I'd be dreaming of ice-skating penguins. I switched to reading at night. Still, I couldn't focus on the meaning. I'd hit a verse I recognized, and I'd be able to hear my own voice saying the verse, somewhere in the past, "But God proves his love for us in that while we were still sinners Christ died for us" (Romans 5:8). Well, there was a verse I recognized. But I couldn't look at it on the page, next to all the other verses, and make the verse *mean* anything. The words had become pure, meaningless sounds.

The book of Ecclesiastes said "All is vanity," but that meant everything *except* the words of the Bible was vanity. These words weren't just supposed to make sense. They were supposed to provide direction for my life.

I didn't tell my parents or my youth pastor what had happened to me. I didn't really know how to describe it. Instead, I kept at it for the rest of the year, and when January first rolled around, in the middle of my senior year of high school, I took the real plunge. I read the whole Bible in a year, Old Testament and all. I added to my regimen a daily journal about my reading, hoping that by writing about the Bible I could force the words to make sense again.

And this time, it went a little better. I actually found myself surprised by sections of the Old Testament. I hadn't realized what jerks most of the kings of Israel were. I hadn't realized how depressed

all the prophets were from watching Jerusalem get razed by one in-
vading horde after another. But my reading of the New Testament
didn't improve. The problem was only compounded by the fact that
I'd started my freshman year at a Christian college, and was taking
a required course in—surprise!—the New Testament. On December
31, I checked the final box on the "Read the Bible in a Year" pamphlet. I folded it and stuck it somewhere in Revelation. And on
January first, when it came time to start my new Bible reading plan,
I just . . . didn't.

Maybe if I'd told my parents or youth pastor about my trouble
with the Bible they'd have been sympathetic. I'd never met a pastor
or church leader who wasn't willing to admit the Bible was a bewildering book; nobody could deny it was full of murders and smitings
and regulations for handling infectious skin diseases, right alongside
the popular inspirational bits. But, the logic went, that weird stuff
was *why* you studied the Bible. There was no such thing as too much
Bible. The more you studied, the more sense it would make, and the
more you'd be able to grow, grow, grow. But even the hardiest of
houseplants will die if overwatered. The more I memorized, read, and
highlighted, the less I seemed to be able to grasp it. Just like I had at
age six, I'd hit the limit for the amount of Bible I could take in.

"The word of God is quick and powerful," sang my mom's friend.
"Sharper than any two-edged sword." Quick, meaning *alive.* My over-
highlighted NIV renders it "living and active," which reminds me of
the label on yogurt: "contains live and active cultures." Living and
active, meaning that the word of God could grow and spread on its
own, quietly and insidiously as the bacteria that turned yogurt into
yogurt. If I was going to read the Bible in any meaningful way, I had
to give all those seeds I'd crammed into my mind a little time to
sprout. So at eighteen, I put the Bible on the shelf for a while. I took
a step back from it, just to see what would happen.

• • •

I'm still taking that step back from the Bible.

Since I checked the last box on my daily Bible reading plan, I've
learned to read New Testament Greek, written some poems about

Bible stories, and explored the Benedictine practice of *lectio divina*, holy reading, where you sit in silence with a text and wait for it to grow on you. I haven't given up the Bible altogether, and I've discovered that there are other ways of reading the Bible besides memorization and a daily quiet time. Yet I've taken up none of these new activities as a regular practice. I guess I'm still afraid a disciplined approach to the Bible will only result in more early morning naps.

Perhaps the most startling thing I've learned over these years is that the Bible is, in fact, a book. This fact may seem obvious, but it dawned on me like the bolt of inspiration my years of daily quiet time had never produced. I've always been an avid reader, and an avid re-reader. It was so freeing for me to realize I could put my Bible on the shelf, like I had done with Nancy Drew or Jane Austen, and take it down whenever I wanted to read the good parts. One day, I might even be able to read some of it for pleasure.

I still expect that the Bible has something to tell me about who God is and how the world is. At the same time, it's no longer the only place I look for God. Sure, I grew in faith and understanding, just as the song promised, but I didn't start shrinking when I stopped reading. Once I started to listen to God's voice beyond just mere words on a page, I realized it had been speaking all along—through my parents' love, through the tall pine trees at camp, through the plain old ordinary books that held me captive—and a whole host of other "worldly" things.

At the Presbyterian church I sometimes attend, neat red Bibles are placed in each pew, each paired with a blue hymnal. There's little rustling of onionskin pages throughout the service. When the lectionary is read, I sometimes look up the passage and read along with the lector. More often, I find myself in that tuned-out state of mind that's become familiar in my encounters with the Bible. I'll find myself staring into space, thinking of nothing, and then I come back to earth with a jolt when the reader proclaims this is "The Word of the Lord."

"Thanks be to God," I say, with everyone else. And sometimes, I think I even mean it.

10

Catholic
Club

by Angie Romines

I've always been a casual, T-shirt and jeans kind of girl. I probably own at least fifty T-shirts. So whichever shirt is singled out among the sea of colored, slightly wrinkled cotton should feel flattered. My favorite T-shirt, which I rescued from the clearance rack at Delia's, has a picture of the Virgin Mary on it. It's that bright color of pink used in candy dyes to entice children, and rests snugly on my frame— with enough soft material to cover my stomach and sleeves cut long so that my arms look much skinnier than they actually are. Under the cartoonish picture of the Virgin, who resembles me, according to my six-year-old brother, is written, "MARY IS MY HOMEGIRL" in bubble letters. The shirt's definitely a conversation piece when I wear it around the campus of my predominantly Protestant college. I usually get one of three reactions: disapproved stares, sputtered laughter, or a tentative, "So are you Catholic or something?" I'll admit it; I love stirring up my otherwise monotonous schedule of chapel, classes, and the occasional Bible study.

But freaking out my classmates is not the only reason I bought my Virgin Mary shirt. The truth is that even though I've never taken the host at Mass or donned a pearl-colored confirmation gown, I still want to feel a little bit Catholic. Maybe it's because of their ancient, alluring rituals, or maybe it's because I've knelt during Mass in their beautiful cathedrals, or maybe it's just because I want to be unabashedly rebellious like some of my Catholic friends. For whatever reason, despite my Protestant educators, I feel connected to the denomination that was conceived two thousand years ago—a denomination that makes Protestants uncomfortable, even though it is the origin of their faith.

Throughout elementary school, I didn't really come in contact with many Catholics. It wasn't until I was eleven and started playing softball that I ever knowingly spoke to one of them. Catholics must love softball because the majority of my little league softball team were baptized as infants with holy water. Those little girls cursed like truck drivers, but I wanted desperately to be accepted by them. They all seemed to have this special "fun aura" around them. I'd never been around such entertaining people who devoured life even as preteens. Their Catholicism was an innate part of who they were—their vocabulary, weekend activities, even their jewelry was touched by their religion. I'd watch Alyssa make the sign of the cross before stepping into the batter's box at each game, hear Katie talk about protesting at the abortion clinic, or flip through pictures of Denise in her confirmation gown, and I'd feel like an outsider—like they had their own little club that had meetings, sing-song chants, and sleepovers that I wasn't allowed to attend.

But the Catholic club wasn't for me because Protestantism was my heritage. My parents were raised in the Pentecostal church, got burned out from incessant services and Bible studies, and so decided sending me to Christian school would teach me five days a week the same values I could get in church—with the added perk that they didn't have to go. Although my parents were tolerant, mild-mannered people, I don't think they would've been overly pleased to know exactly what I was learning.

I attended a Baptist private school from kindergarten through twelfth grade, where I was educated in a variety of subjects—mathematics, creationism, church history with special attention to the Protestant Reformation, which signified the break from the Roman Catholic Church. For the most part, I was taught that Catholics were ridiculous and that if I had any Catholic friends, I should be severely concerned about their entrance into heaven. My teachers would always adopt the same mannerisms, pacing back and forth in front of the white board, hands crooked behind their backs, as they repeated the lectures that I'm sure their parents passed down to them.

Now class, we all agree that Mother Teresa was a very good person. She tended to the poor and lived a life of service in India, but did she go to heaven? (This was the point where they always paused and scanned the room to be certain their words were being absorbed.) *Maybe not.* (Knowing eye contact with the back row.) *Catholics like Mother Teresa think that you can buy salvation through good deeds. We all hope she accepted Jesus as her Savior, but we can't be sure.*

Listening to the same speech spoken from different pursed lips year after year instilled a slight disdain for Catholicism in me. What a ridiculous religion to believe in—purgatory, saints, and priests— honestly. But still, I listened intently whenever my Bible or history teachers covered Catholic history or traditions in class. It was as if by studying their ceremonies, crusades, and customs, I could seep into the Catholic world and loosen the restraints of Protestant piety that surrounded me. Maybe it's because Catholicism was presented as the forbidden fruit. I longed for the cloying taste in my mouth— the same rich flavor on my tongue as when classes became too boring my classmates and I would comb through the Old Testament to the "scandalous" parts—the mass circumcisions, the prostitute being carved into twelve pieces.

But even though my softball teammates' carefree, cursing-filled lifestyle tempted me like those secret passages of Scripture, I still had Protestant indoctrination ingrained in my head. I believed every acrid word that dropped from my teachers' mouths because they appeared to possess superhuman morals—they projected infallibility. They went to church every Sunday, dressed neatly, and always said "rear end" instead of "ass" like my Catholic pals. *Confessing on schedule and hailing Mary when appropriate doesn't get you into heaven,* I thought; the countless lectures and fear of the burning lake of fire cemented my doubt in Catholicism.

As I grew up and female elementary school teachers were traded up for male junior high and high school teachers, I began to realize why my esteemed Christian educators preached so fervently about how living a good life doesn't get you into heaven. It seemed obvious that they would choose the religion that did not hold them directly accountable for their secrets. Why list out your embarrassing, vile sins to a priest, when it was so much easier to hide behind the Protestant façade of after-church potlucks and "Jesus is my co-pilot" bumper stickers? All you needed was a trim wife, athletic kids, and a Republican voting record, and you could shatter just about any commandment of your choice within the tight-knit evangelical community.

Mr. Vandell was an über-Protestant who attended my school as a student before coming back to teach junior high history, geography, and some primary algebra. I can't really remember anything specific he taught me because he wasn't a good teacher. Most fifty-minute class periods were spent answering trivia questions and trying to shoot a miniature foam Pacers basketball into a trash can on the opposite side of the classroom. But I do remember how stiff and chilled I felt, like an ice cube had been tucked into the back of my shirt, as he leaned over my chair and whispered the answers to test questions into my ear. Don't be alarmed. I wasn't singled out. That's just how he taught girls. I also remember how he interrupted his own lesson about Sumerian writing utensils to inform us we'd fill out our shirts someday, and then boys would start to notice us.

It took until I was just shy of sixteen for Mr. Vandell's prophecy to come true. Out of nowhere, the same shirt that hung like a loose pillowcase when I was in junior high now clung tightly to my chest like a bathing suit. I was pretty oblivious until strangers started looking me over like a slab of steak, and my guy friends went from punching me on my arm to goosing me while I rifled through the contents of my overcrowded locker. I learned fast not to bend over without making a full 360-degree sweep of the vicinity for predators.

It was around this time that I enrolled in a Driver's Ed class at Our Lady of the Immaculate Conception, one of my city's Catholic high schools. I didn't know a single soul in the 350-person class; they had known each other as classmates for years. The seating chart placed me next to Melissa Samsa, a blue-eyed brunette who seemed to know anyone who was worth knowing at Our Lady. I thought she looked much older than her fifteen years. I wasn't the only one who thought so, because she told me the management at Hooters had offered her a job last time she had stopped in with her friends for some wings. She used to come to class every morning hung over and full of fantastic tales. I was learning more about the delicate art of beer-bonging and how to curse in acronyms than I was about stick shifts and turn signals.

By the end of the three-week session, I had managed to secure a tentative place in Mel's tight circle—which was probably due to the fact that I was such an easily entertained and shocked listener. During our last class, she and her in-crowd Catholic friends tried to convince me to transfer to Our Lady. I considered it for the better part of three minutes, but truthfully, their wild lifestyles were too intimidating for me. Plus, it was a little late in the game for me to relearn the politics of a new school and denomination. It was embarrassing enough to mumble slurred syllables of the Hail Mary each morning at Driver's Ed because I didn't know the words beyond "full of grace." Our Lady was too foreign, too alive for me to thrust myself in without even knowing how to pray correctly. I was comfortable with Protestant school and its predictable hypocrites and familiar routine to risk flinging myself into the unknown halls of Catholic high school.

If I had donned the plaid skirt and collared uniform shirt at Our Lady, I wouldn't have been back at my Protestant school sitting in Mr. Graceton's class. Mr. Graceton, who twitched his mouth to the left when he spoke, trying to mask his chipped front tooth, taught my Bible class. But I use the term "taught" loosely. An example question from one of his less-than-challenging exams:

> 17. Identify the gospel trio.
>   a. faith, hope, and love
>   b. sin, death, and dispair
>   c. Phillips, Craig, and Dean

Along with teaching Bible, Mr. Graceton was also the school's disciplinary administrator. He doled out detentions for those who asked to go to the bathroom too many times. After all, too many interruptions would take away from the weight and poignancy of his lecture-sermons. Suspensions were reserved for the wayward teens who sampled their parents' wine coolers and turned themselves in during a fit of guilt. They most likely would've kept this sin a secret had Mr. Graceton not passed out blank sheets of paper and instructed us to write down whatever unsavory activities we knew our friends were involved in. He saved the expulsions for the rebellious freshmen boys who split a bottle of Tyler McDowell's morphine prescription in the second-floor men's room. And on rare occasions, he would be forced to paddle those boys whose parents just didn't love them enough to "spank them straight."

While the girls (as an unspoken understanding) didn't have to fear Mr. Graceton's wooden paddle, they did have to sit through a dress-code assembly and hear the phrase, "You girls are making it hard to be a male teacher around here." Apparently some of us were pushing the "sleeveless is okay, but tank tops are not" rule too far. Right after the assembly, the girls from my grade and I headed to the locker room to change for gym. We did so quickly, almost quick enough to block out the image of Mr. Graceton and the other male teachers watching us undress in their minds. Apparently, Mr. Vandell had been right about our tops filling out.

Because of "pious" teachers like Mr. Vandell and Mr. Graceton, it's surprising that I would be drawn to a denomination that lifts up a single man to sit on earth as God's supreme authority. But I admit feeling a little lost when I first heard Pope John Paul II had passed away. I pitied the orphaned Catholic Church—probably grief-stricken and feeling the abandonment and panic that sets in after the death of a parent. The Catholic children must have been stunned—caught with cans of beer in their hands as the sheriff gently broke the news that tilted the rhythm of their riotous lives. I felt a little guilty mourning with them, like an uninvited funeral guest, an outsider who didn't really know the deceased but felt the need to include herself anyway.

I've always liked Pope John Paul II. Actually I don't know much about him at all other than that he was older than bedrock and Polish instead of the usual Italian. And I only learned this after he received his last rites. I think I might like the idea of a pope more than the actual pope himself: a father figure, righteous and infallible in matters of the church—at least according to my Catholic friends. I'm sure that John Paul II, or Karol, as his mother named him, drank too much sacramental wine on occasion or committed murder in his heart against the Nazi soldiers who closed down seminaries and ravaged his Polish countryside and people during World War II. I'm not naive enough to think John Paul II was human perfection walking the earth; popes are made of bones and flesh, too. The Catholics have their fallen, especially within the priesthood. But I have a feeling that if I had traveled to the Vatican before he died and had knelt before him awaiting the papal blessing, he wouldn't have tried to look down my top.

I haven't really talked to Theresa, my closest Catholic friend, since Pope John Paul died. A considerate person probably would have sent sympathies when the human cornerstone of a good friend's religion had moved on to a higher spiritual plane, but I've been busy. I met Theresa while working with her in the children's department at the library during my summers home from college. Theresa isn't just Catholic; she's super Catholic. Confession at least once every three months, Catholic high school (Our Lady) and college, house doused in religious memorabilia, and plus, her mom's name is Mary Margaret.

Theresa and I became close because we discovered we both have a penchant for sarcasm and live half a mile away from each other, so we carpooled to work. Sometimes on those twenty-minute car rides home, I'd reinstate the Spanish Inquisition and ask her all about Catholicism. I'd ask her about what she said in confession, how purgatory worked, and the words to the Hail Mary. Usually, she was willing to satisfy my curiosity by answering all my questions patiently and without taking offense. She even took me to Mass with her several times without me having to beg too much.

During winter break one year, after a Saturday-night Mass service, Theresa coerced me into attending an after-church party with her. Going to Mass and watching the beautiful rituals as a spectator was much different than socializing in a party setting with a large group of people who all had the commonality of beliefs. The gathering was held at a large house on the outskirts of the city, and I've never felt so claustrophobic. It was impossible to walk two inches without nearly crushing one of the hundreds of children scuttling in between grown-ups' legs. Everyone had a glass of wine in their hand, and even though I was underage and driving that night, they (meaning some of the mothers and fathers) tried to get me to join them in their boisterous festivities. By politely refusing, I marked myself as an outsider right away. They looked at me as if trying to figure out how nature could have crafted someone so different from themselves.

I didn't make the same mistake when I visited Theresa at her Catholic college. Saint Joseph's was an ancient campus—in terms of American history—with buildings dating back to the 1800s, when nuns tried to convert the pagan Native Americans by sending them to missionary schools. Theresa informed me that the buildings that used to be part of the mission were haunted, and at the time, I was drunk enough to believe her. Apparently, Catholic colleges are able to claim to be dry campuses but still have a fully-stocked bar in the basement beneath the cafeteria. I was incredibly underage and never should have been granted admission, let alone given free drinks all night. It felt nice to not be immediately picked off as the Protestant outsider. With a drink in my hand, no one knew I'd never taken First Communion. I blended into them; I finally accomplished what I had been trying all those years ago at softball practice and Driver's Ed classes. Even though I was living outside the Protestant law at the time, I relished every second of "Catholic time" I got to spend with Theresa. It was as if by slipping into her Catholic world, I had managed to crack into a snow globe without any of the perpetually smiling villagers noticing my presence.

But my Protestant training has caught up with me as it always does. Since tasting that brief moment of acceptance at Theresa's college, I've set down my shot glass and earnestly tried to blend back into my evangelical Christian college. It's just easier that way—fewer questions, fewer consequences, fewer confrontations (in brotherly love, of course). But every three weeks or so, I slide into my Virgin Mary T-shirt with wicked mischief in my eyes, awaiting the Protestant shock that is sure to ensue. It's my own minuscule rebellion, like double piercing my ears instead of going straight for the lip ring. I strut around campus as heads whip around to read the text beneath the Virgin's upturned palms, and I feel a fleeting bit of triumph. Or maybe the feeling is nothing more than a small consolation—for being born Protestant instead of Catholic.

11

Dead
End

by Jessica Belt

I visited the Haji Ali Mosque for the first and only time when I was nineteen, with a group of Americans researching Indian religions. The Mumbai shore was stifling in the summer days before the heavens would release onto the parched Indian soil. I weaved through a crowd toward a causeway that extends into the Arabian Sea for nearly a mile, ending at the mosque. The path was congested with pilgrims going there and back again: men with glossy raven-colored hair, women who concealed themselves modestly with cotton head cloths.

Balancing on my tiptoes, I craned to see Murli, our Indian tour guide. *There*—I spotted him not too far ahead. I lowered my heels and meandered along at the pace of the crowd, unhurried for once.

Mumbai wasn't just mesmerizing, it was dizzying. I'd turn a street corner and in a single breath, inhale coriander, marijuana, and urine. In the same step, I'd dodge a careening rickshaw and a cow with two humps along its back. Photos of Bollywood beauties were plastered on roadside porn stands. Children chased their friends, laughing and ducking in and out of the crowds. Police officers stood around, thumbs tucked in their pockets. The clouds would burst any day now, bringing the monsoon. My own hands and feet were hennaed in patterns of paisleys that expanded across my Anglo skin into flowers, suns, and birds.

"Hello! Good day, Madam!" a vendor called to me. "You want something? Lovely gifts! Only 350 rupees."

The fat man waved a trinket. At the stand to his right, a group of women exchanged rupees for small floral offerings. The fat vendor didn't sell offerings, but he pointed to the faded postcards and bottles of water that filled his stand. My face felt flushed. Were these the unsealed bottles that had been filled at the local rivers? The bottles Murli warned us not to touch to our lips?

"No, thank you. Not today." I shook my head, but my polite reply was ignored as he yelled again, his voice carrying across the crowd.

As I stepped from the mainland, my sandals slid on the causeway's slippery cement. The causeway stood no more than a foot above the water line, and it was barely wide enough to hold ten people standing side by side. Aluminum cans, swollen cardboard, and various unidentifiable forms of rubbish bobbed along the water's surface. Virginia, my childhood friend, slid on the slime, grabbing my arm to steady herself. I looked back and gave her a weary smile.

During high tide, the waters would swell and cover the causeway so that the mosque appeared to float on the sea. The illusion bears testament to Muslim businessman-turned-saint Haji Ali, whose casket is said to have miraculously floated from Mecca back to Mumbai, and whose remains lie beneath the marble floor. I craned to see the mosque, but I could only glimpse the upper edges of its whitewashed walls, punctuated with spired minarets. In the distance, women wearing saris reclined on a neighboring stretch of beach and children splashed in the muddy waves. People all around me stepped slowly and solemnly.

The path across the sea was a juncture, one of East and West, sacred and secular, ambition and fate. There, even gods collided: Krishna, Allah, Vishnu, Christ. The deities were why I had come. The group I traveled with was sent by a Christian church to research Indian religions, intending one day to use our findings to win converts. I had also hoped to hear a calling, some divinely inspired purpose that would carry me through life.

Waves lapped against the walkway, coating the asphalt with a slick film. Several paces ahead of me, Murli pointed upward toward the mosque, no doubt to divulge some little-known fact about Haji Ali or practicing Islam in India, but I could not hear what he said.

Murli's wealthy Hindu parents and brother had converted to Christianity when he was a young man, but he resisted until his father pleaded with him to read the Bible. Eventually, Murli renounced the gods of his childhood for Jesus. Now he is married to the daughter of a prominent Indian evangelical missionary, and he teaches at a seminary in southern India. His religious tours are popular with Indians and Westerners alike because, as he said, his face cannot be *placed*. Peasants often approach him as if he's from their village; wealthy urbanites assume that he is of their caste. Murli has mastered some of the more widely-spoken languages, and perhaps most importantly, locals tell him that he resembles a popular Bollywood actor.

Already this morning, Murli had taken us to three temples: the Jain, where meticulous men wearing loincloths sat on their haunches and patterned rice on a board; a large Hindu temple, where I placed my rubber flip-flops among a row of sandals and wished for an offering to lay at the gods' gilded feet; and afterwards, a smaller Hindu temple, where I kept my shoes on and sneaked behind the building to watch waves crash against the rocks. In his childhood home of Mumbai, Murli navigated the temples effortlessly. He could convince any temple guard to allow inside a giggling group of young Americans. He knew when to crack a joke, when to tell a secret. Yet he led more quickly than I wanted to follow.

At each holy site I created stories of other journeyers—of pregnant mothers with their husbands, of clusters of young and old, and of solitary travelers. They all seemed to me unexpectedly, unwaveringly devoted. Some carried elaborate offerings. Others whispered prayers, rocked their torsos forward and back, or moved their hands and arms in sequenced acts of worship.

The Haji Ali was both a landmark and a holy site, though for the most part, I could not distinguish between worshippers and tourists. Most of the journeyers walked in silence. For Muslims from southeast Asia throughout centuries, the trek to Haji Ali has been an important pilgrimage. The journey is often made in preparation for a longer pilgrimage to Mecca. Ahead of me, a couple of Americans chatted loudly about sweat stains. I rolled my eyes, almost certain that they were part of my group. I lagged further behind to try to blend in with the pilgrims.

When I had said goodbye to my parents at the airport, they hugged me and said simply, "Remember to come home, Jessica." I hugged them back but didn't respond. On the airplane, Virginia and I had joked over our dinners of microwaved potato curry that we might decide to stay in India. We were giddy with wanderlust. Neither of us had ever before traveled outside of the U.S., though we'd often talked of picking up and moving somewhere far away. Ever since we were girls, we had wanted to be Christian missionaries—she to somewhere in southern Asia, me to northern Africa. The two-week trip to India was an aptitude test.

Months before we left, Virginia and I had written letters to our friends and family to fundraise. We met regularly with others from the church to pray and prepare Bible lessons for a youth camp we all would lead near the seminary where Murli taught. I pored over a book about Amy Carmichael, an Englishwoman who in the early twentieth century had opened a home to protect orphan girls from being prostituted at temples. When people would ask her why she gave up her life in England for colonial India, she declared that it was in service to her god.

Even when I boarded the plane, I thought I shared her faithfulness.

Of the three Abrahamic faiths, only Christians do not observe a commission to return to a physical place that roots their faith. When the Jewish people of the Bible are exiled time and again, the prophets of the Hebrew Scriptures remind them not to forget Jerusalem. Though I've not studied the Qur'an, I imagine that the journey to Mecca offers to followers of Allah a similar hope: for peace, unity, and a home where the spiritual and physical worlds can co-exist. Yet Christians throughout history have gone forth into the world, obeying the final command of the resurrected Christ. Jesus himself left his home in Nazareth and asked his followers to forsake even their mothers and fathers to follow him. Perhaps the greatest symbol of devotion in evangelical Christianity is to leave one's country and preach the gospel, without plans to ever return.

As I shuffled along the causeway, wishing for even a sip of water to trickle down my dry throat, I felt a brush against my ankle. I looked down to see a legless beggar pleading for a few rupees. I had been forbidden by the church leaders to give away money, since it could attract pickpockets' attention. What else did I have to give? If I were to bend and whisper a prayer in the beggar's ear, I might be praised, maybe even written about in a brochure for the church's next trip to India. No, this man needed food and money and medical attention. The Englishwoman who sheltered orphan girls would have known how to ease his pain, even if the comfort lasted only for a moment. But I had nothing useful to offer him, so I turned away.

I wiped my temple with the back of my hand, smearing sweat into my hair. My nose and cheeks burned, and I hadn't thought to bring along sunscreen. What *was* I doing here?

"Were your boogers black this morning?" I heard someone ask.

"What?" I replied and saw Virginia next to me.

"Come on, admit it," she coaxed. "Everyone else's were."

For as long as I could remember, Virginia had told me odd little bodily myths that I wanted to believe, even if I knew better. She once insisted that if she spent enough time in the summer sun, her freckles would melt together, dark and smooth, a surfacing of the Cherokee blood flowing beneath her spotty Anglo-Saxon skin. When we had sleepovers, we named freckle constellations: Grandpa's Nose, the Ant. We found a crescent moon that waxed just below the bend in her elbow. I never remembered the constellations, but Virginia could find them again and again. She claimed that her galaxy was expanding, and I was never sure that she was wholly kidding.

"I didn't have boogers today," I lied and drifted toward the causeway's edge.

A wave crashed against the side of the stone, spraying me with sewage-tainted water. I lifted the bottom of my *salwar kameez* to wipe my face. I had purchased the outfit the previous day between temple visits. Jet-lagged and culture-shocked, we had all craved familiarity. Murli suggested shopping. "It always cheers up Americans," he smiled. By the end of the afternoon, everyone wore brightly colored saris or tunics, and I hadn't even felt guilty for living up to my consumerist stereotype. I now felt more exposed with my costume than

I would have if I had been wearing everyday jeans and a T-shirt. Muslim Indians adorned themselves in less decorative attire than Hindus did. The orange embroidered flowers along the trim of my tunic were just as out of place as my uncovered braids whipping brazenly in the wind.

The mosque seemed somehow to grow more hidden as I neared it. I peeked between the heads of the people in front of me but I could barely see the walls. They seemed taller than before, almost completely obstructing my view of the palms and minarets. The muezzin's song-prayers rang out, drawing the crowd irresistibly. The pace quickened. Eager worshippers pressed upon me, and almost before I realized my journey had ended, I squeezed through a tall and narrow gate.

The crowd thinned quickly and I took in a deep breath, the first not laden with smells of sewage and human odor. A breeze glided across the nape of my neck and cooled me momentarily. I welcomed the respite of slowing down. Of personal space. Why analyze the peace? Why raise further questions?

Virginia and the others in our group followed Murli toward a small garden. I lagged a few steps behind, gravel crunching softly under my sandals. Knee-high palms and broad-leafed hostas grew in a carefully manicured strip along the edge of the mosque. Asymmetrical patches of green dotted the courtyard. There were few flowers. Instead, the landscape was made intricate through textures: sturdy tropical leaves, veiny variegations, lacy ferns. The flora was accented with trickling fountains and stone benches where people sat to rest or pray.

Murli stopped next to a statue, presumably of Haji Ali himself. When Haji Ali gave up his business and set out for Mecca, had he felt called there by his god? He was already an old man at the time he had left Mumbai. When he reached Mecca, how long had he planned to stay?

Devotees crowded around the statue and pushed gently to stand nearer to it. Before I could get a good look, Murli turned away and led us to a clearing. We huddled together, ready for instructions. I stood in the back, half-listening and watching how the masses of worshippers diffused as soon as they passed through the gate. Some walked quietly and purposefully, as if pilgrimaging to Haji Ali was as familiar as kneeling toward Mecca. Others paused only a few feet inside the courtyard, looking up and around, forcing those behind them to pass on the left or right.

The walls of the mosque curved, and it appeared as if there might have been more than one building. I leaned back to peer around the façade and tried to guess where Murli would lead us first. Are there places that we wouldn't be allowed to visit? Would Murli convince someone to let us through? Virginia grasped my elbow, pulling me back into the group. "Stay close," she whispered. I felt a little guilty for tuning out and tried to refocus, but Murli had stopped talking.

"What's happening?" I asked Virginia, my eyebrows furrowed. She shushed me and pointed at Murli. He was silent and alert. His eyes darted side to side, and he motioned us to pull in closer toward him. I moved a half step forward, not wanting to press too close against other sweaty bodies. Was there danger? Most of the worshippers ignored us completely as they migrated from the statue to the mosque's entrances at the back of the courtyard.

"Keep together," I heard an American snap. Murli turned abruptly and hurried back toward the gate.

"What's the rush?" I said, looking toward the mosque. "Why are we leaving?" Of course, I had wanted to stay longer in the courtyard. And of course, I'd hoped to take my time once I was inside to study the colors and mosaic patterns. Over my shoulder, though, I saw some men in dark cotton pants whispering to one another and looking towards us. They appeared harmless. Murli wove through the courtyard. I jogged a few steps to catch up. Did we have to leave only minutes after we had arrived? Again, I looked over my shoulder. The men still followed a few paces behind. Just then, one of the men shouted a guttural, alarming cry.

The entrails of paradise churned, as if to vomit us out. We escaped through the gate. Back on the causeway, at the back of the group, I trudged as slowly as Murli would permit. We shoved past worshippers, hurrying too quickly, too fearfully. We retraced our steps, sliding again through the muck, past the devout, the dutiful, the dying. I searched for something to report. Back home, I might have mentioned the beggars and the vendors, the friction between poverty and wealth, lingering remnants of the caste system. I might have spoken of rejection, why we hurried away from the mosque as if we had mistakenly wound up at a dead end on the wrong side of town.

I arrived in India presuming that my god is superior: He. Is. Superior. But my research suggested otherwise. In India, God is both he and she; is and is not; exists immeasurably above, beyond, below, and around. God is paradox. Or is it that Paradox is divine?

Most of the worshippers and tourists I passed would have disagreed with my presumptions. More than five hundred million gods are worshipped in India. Some people, like the Muslim pilgrims, worshipped only one god. Others worshipped many. Some even created their own gods at local design-your-own-idol shops and built shrines to their personalized deities. The rice-patterners at the Jain temple did not worship any god at all; they pursued the spiritual to learn peace and self-control. In such a religious cacophony, not only was my god not superior, he may have been irrelevant.

The truth is, I could not report what I had seen without also reporting about myself, about how belief itself seemed as slippery as the causeway. I stared hard into the eyes of the devotees passing me, envying that they seemed to journey toward a sacred and assured destination. When I'd left the United States, I made the mistake of thinking that I would be an ambassador, not a pilgrim. But my pilgrimage had begun. It was a journey not to, but from. I was not bringing answers, but facing questions.

Of course, my parents expected me to return home. But is home itself an illusion, like a floating mosque? On their pilgrimages, even the faithful—once they had reached Haji Ali and had prayed and given their offerings—they, like me, would have to turn around and retrace their steps. They would return to their homes and sweep and bake bread. In the mundane, too, they are asked to be faithful: to kneel and pray five times daily, to reserve one day each week for worship with their community.

Though my god did not require me to complete specific spiritual tasks, the church encouraged me to pray and read the Bible daily if possible. For most of my life, I had done my best to be faithful. But it was the command to go forth into the world that had captivated me. It was a commission I wanted to fulfill. Would a grander effort land me closer to God?

I stepped off of the causeway, returning to dry ground. After a grueling journey across the desert, Haji Ali's casket just floated across the ocean back to the place where he was conceived. For all we know, even he wasn't aware where he finally came to rest.

From a distance, places can appear holier or more needy of salvation than they really are. I resisted the urge to turn my head and look back at the Haji Ali Mosque, the lovely stepchild of Indian enchantment and Islamic devotion. Up ahead, Virginia already stood on the mainland. Her back faced me, her hair whipping in the sea breeze. I could tell she was laughing as if she believed she was safe from whatever danger had faced us, and I wished that she wasn't. I wanted her to agree that we perhaps hadn't known where we were going all along, from the time we boarded the plane. But Virginia had always adopted myths easily, proclaiming them as if they were the hard and fast truth. Though her claims were at least in part for love of debate, I never knew whether she also really, literally believed what she professed.

As for me, I no longer knew what to believe.

12

Surviving the
Call
to
Missions

by Kirsten Cruzen

The piano notes started softly at first, just below the rumble of the pastor's closing prayer, and then intensified at the "Amen." Roused by the message or the promise of afternoon football, the congregation rose to its feet and sang out:

> All to Jesus, I surrender;
> All to him I freely give;
> I will ever love and trust him,
> In his presence daily live.

I soaked in the intimacy of singing with my church family, rocking back and forth with the simple melody. We took a deep breath and in full volume started the refrain. I opened my mouth wide to sing the high note "I," holding it for two counts before skipping through the beats in "surrender" and ending at the "ah" sound in "all." Then again, "I surrender all. All to thee, my blessed Savior," and one last time, "I surrender all."

Then I noticed my mom had gone silent. This puzzled me until I remembered that she had recently told my dad, "I opened my mouth to sing, and I just couldn't make myself say the words. I kept thinking, 'I don't surrender all, Jesus.'" Knowing how hard my mom

107

worked to surrender her life to Jesus, I wondered if I dare sing the words. Was I capable of surrendering it all?

That November, the year I turned eleven, my family attended an orientation program run by Wycliffe Bible Translators, the mission organization my parents wanted to join. For four weeks, my family of five lived in a tiny two-room cabin while Wycliffe missionaries simulated the stresses of missionary life. My two younger brothers and I home-schooled with a few other children, and my parents took linguistic, doctrine, and anthropology courses. I understood that if my parents passed the classes and Wycliffe approved our family, then we would become missionaries, which would make me a missionary kid, an MK.

During that month, I began to learn what surrendering all would mean. If we were accepted, we would spend years moving so my parents could be trained for the mission field and then eventually move to Africa. My father would give up his guaranteed salary as a manager with Fluor Daniel. I would leave the only house I remembered, my grandparents, my friends, my status and security in the gifted and talented program at school, and my first crush. My brothers loved the promise of adventure, but I just wanted life to stay the same. I felt safe in Southern California—successful at school and piano lessons, known by teachers, surrounded by friends and loved by my Evangelical Free Church community. Why couldn't we be like the other people we knew at church who could love Jesus without surrendering all?

I responded to the stresses and doubts of that month by coming down with the stomach flu three times. But my parents and the Wycliffe counselors considered this part of the MK growing process. During the last week, one of the counselors asked to speak with me privately. I knew this had something to do with our official acceptance, and I contemplated saying something horrendous about my family in the hopes that Wycliffe would refuse us. Instead, I was honest with him about not wanting to be a missionary kid. The counselor told me stories about how his kids adjusted to being MKs and assured me one day I would come to like it. That was the adult consensus: I would get used to it.

We returned to our home in Anaheim in December. I had six months to say goodbye and sort through the material accumulations of my childhood. My parents had six months to raise a new source of income from churches and friends who would promise to send us money each month. As they began sharing their testimonies with potential supporters, I learned more about why this was happening to me.

God had called my mother first. She heard God tell her in an audible voice, "This is the work I have for you," while watching a movie about mission work in her Bible Study Fellowship class. Hearing God's voice in anything but quiet whispers to the heart was not part of my Christian community's experience. It meant my mother was either crazy, mistaken, or that God *really, really* wanted us to be missionaries. Everyone seemed to think it was the last option.

At the same time, my father was also noticing messages about missions in his Bible readings, but he wasn't so anxious to follow the call. Eventually he felt that God gave him a choice between the desires of his heart or the desires of God's heart. Whittled down to such bare desires, my dad chose God's path.

They chose Wycliffe Bible Translators because they felt the Bible had played such an important role in their own faith lives. My mom often quoted Revelation 7:9: "After this I looked and there was a great multitude that no one could count, from every nation, from all tribes and peoples and languages, standing before the throne and before the Lamb." Wycliffe focuses on the "all tribes and peoples and languages" portion of this verse. If every language is to be represented in front of the throne one day, they reason, then every language needs the Bible—the Christian New Testament at the very least.

I believed we had to obey God, but that didn't relieve my anger and grief. I tried to finish up my fifth-grade year normally, but some things couldn't be ignored. Mom began to go through the house, purging, boxing, and selling. Then in the spring, a missionary family serving in Ireland came to our church for a visit. They had a boy my age.

"Hi, I'm a missionary kid," he announced proudly in my Sunday school class.

My teachers smiled enthusiastically, and I glared at him. He wore a sweater vest and answered questions in Sunday school eagerly and earnestly. I was determined not to like him, which wasn't hard because my friends all kept their distance. Our parents and teachers were impressed by his family's devotion to God, but that didn't cause him to win the respect of my peers.

For me, his presence raised very complicated feelings. In just a few months, I was going to be the stranger in a new church. I was going to be the missionary kid. I watched him try to fit in with the other boys, but he didn't know how to skateboard. He tried to make up for his awkwardness with stories about his life in Ireland. He told his stories in a bragging tone that annoyed my friends, but I secretly marveled at his pride. How could he so easily embody the stereotype of an MK? Couldn't he see he didn't belong?

My parents stayed late after church to glean wisdom from his parents' experiences. They told me I should ask the boy about life as an MK. I was horrified. Didn't my parents see it? He was a complete and total *nerd*! I wouldn't be caught dead talking to him. And he *liked* being a missionary kid. I was never going to be like him. Never.

Despite my resistance, we moved once the school year ended. My school friends threw me a going away party and promised to write. Our house was emptied and rented out to strangers. My dad attached a small red trailer to the back of our minivan, and for two months, we trekked across the country in search of supporters.

After the support-raising trip, my parents took a required year of linguistic courses at the Wycliffe Center in Dallas. Though I met other MKs in the Wycliffe housing area, it was a lonely year. I wallpapered my room with letters from home and tried to pretend that I still belonged to those groups.

Then we left Dallas, put eight thousand more miles on the van during a second summer of support-raising, and ended our travels at the Wycliffe missionary center outside of Charlotte, North Carolina. Since my father would be working with computers and not translating Bibles, he needed four months of additional training.

As soon as we arrived in North Carolina, my brothers went outside on their bikes and were swimming at the community pool in a matter of hours. I retreated with my books to my new room, unsure of how to approach the other kids I noticed from my window. I was prepared to continue with my strategy of withdrawal, but then someone invited me swimming.

That first day at the pool I met Ashlea, the daughter of a Baptist preacher. We shared the same birthday and were both going into seventh grade. She quickly started including me in her plans for the upcoming school year. I warmed at the attention, hungry for acceptance. With Ashlea at my side, I overcame my fear of rejection and met the many teenagers who made up the missionary center youth group. The teenagers met weekly on Thursday nights for Bible study, where we flirted, laughed, and studied the holy Word of God. For the first time in more than a year, I belonged again.

I grew closest to Ashlea and the three Altork sisters (ages sixteen, thirteen, and eleven) who lived in the apartment building next to mine. The Altork girls' father was a former pastor, and like Ashlea's father, he was from a Christian denomination that was much more conservative than my parents'. Suddenly I was participating in doctrinal debates like whether salvation was a once-and-for-all transaction or something that could be lost. At a sleepover one night, we stayed up reading Revelation, trying to figure out if Christians were going to be called into heaven in a rapture or have to stay and endure the end times with the sinners. We ended our readings convinced that post-tribulation rapture was the only correct reading of Revelation, and I went home to inform my parents of the difficulties that awaited us as Christians.

I was also observing new moral restrictions. My new friends believed dancing was a sin. We were cautious with our clothing and makeup, mindful that our purity be reflected in our appearance. Our sexuality was dangerous, a temptation that required constant vigilance to control.

For this reason, we weren't supposed to watch movies with sexuality in them. Older movies were popular in Ashlea's family, because those movies represented a time when our culture wasn't so corrupt. Or at least her family convinced themselves of this. One night we all watched the Doris Day movie *Pillow Talk*, about a womanizer who eventually wins Doris Day's heart. At one point, when Doris Day thinks to herself "make love to me," while they were driving to

Rock Hudson's country cabin, Ashlea's sister interrupted the movie to announce that back in the fifties when people said "make love" it meant "make out."

These expressions of piety were important because we were called to be separate from the world—a light on a hill. Through our pure, exemplary lives, we could save lost souls. The idea of being set apart appealed to me. I was already set apart by my parents' life choices. It was redeeming to have that otherness become a mark of honor.

During this time and surrounded by these friends, I began to construct a story about myself and God to help me make sense of the pain and sorrow I had experienced since my parents had joined missions. I told myself that I used to be a selfish, proud girl, that God had to take that life away from me so that I could be humbled and learn to trust completely in him. I began to identify with my mother's desire to surrender all. I embraced my faith radically and vigilantly. My friends and I challenged each other to remember Jesus's imminent return. Would we be ready? Would we have saved enough souls?

When we left North Carolina, we returned to California to prepare to leave for France and Africa. Returning to California made me realize how much I had changed. A year earlier I longed to see my friends, but now, I didn't even contact the school friends I had known all of my life. I didn't think I would have anything in common with them.

When our home church in California commissioned my parents six months later, my brothers and I were called up onto the stage with them. The elders of the church surrounded us and laid their hands on us, and then our friends and my grandparents stood behind them, reaching in to touch us. The pastor prayed for our blessing and protection. We were sent forth, and although I couldn't say no, it no longer mattered. I was now willing to do my part for the lost souls of the world.

During my eighteen months in France, I imagined myself to be an ambassador for Christ in a culture that had obviously fallen into the clutches of the devil. And then I fell in love with that culture. It happened slowly, but after attending French school, worshiping in a

French evangelical church, and exploring Europe with my family, I started to love the French way of life.

Unfortunately, we needed to adjust to African culture, not French culture, to serve on the mission field. When my family ended our language training in France, we traveled to Yaoundé, Cameroon for "Africa Orientation"—three months of anthropology, health, and practical living classes designed to help missionaries adjust to the challenges of living in Africa.

I was the only high school student at the training, so for a challenge, I joined the anthropology course with the adults. The conversations that came up in this class stretched my thinking. A German missionary asked about going topless in the villages where this was standard for the African women. The American women were appalled at the suggestion, but it made me think, "Why not?" Why was it okay for some cultures and not okay for others?

The teacher required us to keep a detailed journal of cultural observations and experiences, and she would read and comment on them. When I made observations about how "lost" different people were, she responded with gentle comments about that being true, but not the purpose of the journal. The journal was for observations without judgment; she wanted me to see through my preconceptions. Keeping the journal forced me to think objectively and to find explanations other than God's will to understand the world around me.

When the three months of training in Cameroon was over, we finally moved to Abidjan, Ivory Coast. After years of training and moving, we had finally reached the point where my parents could begin their full-time work as missionaries. My father managed the computer services for the branch. My mother was the education co-ordinator, which meant she made sure all of the MKs in the branch received an appropriate education.

We began preparing for the start of the next school year, and I learned that many of the MKs from other mission organizations went to a missionary boarding school five hours north of Abidjan, in a town called Bouaké. I saw this as an opportunity to live out my faith surrounded by MKs once again. It also provided the possibility of having a boyfriend. And since my convictions only allowed me to date a Christian, the lack of Christians my age at the International School in Abidjan concerned me. I begged my parent to send me away, which they resisted, loath to see me so far away, but they left the final decision to me.

Living at this boarding school put me under the authority of fundamentalist doctrines and rules in a way that I hadn't previously experienced. Even though I'd seen conservative doctrine in action in North Carolina, at boarding school, I was completely under its authority, as opposed to voluntarily imposing restrictions that were meaningful to me. The collective weekly meeting of "dorm dads" determined the "biblical" rules we students lived by; the men (and only the men) took turns preaching each Sunday, and the women were sure to reinforce the understanding that it was the man's role to be the spiritual leader. Spending time alone with a member of the opposite sex was considered a "date" and was forbidden except during "dating" hours. All physical contact between boys and girls was forbidden, and we were taught in our Sex Ed class that men had trouble controlling themselves, so it was the woman's responsibility to guard her virginity and maintain the boundaries in a relationship. Music and movies were tightly controlled—we had to turn in the lyrics of every song that we brought onto campus, and any other music found in our room was considered contraband.

The challenges that these rules and doctrines would present to my faith were not apparent to me initially. These teachings and rules were presented to me as "biblical," a convenient category that imbued the staff with God's authority, and I had entered this new school anxious to please the God I had come to know, encouraged by the devotion that I saw in the Christian students around me. I participated soulfully in the spiritual emphasis weeks, confessing my sins, looking for ways to purify myself before God. And I joined Evangelism Explosion, a door-to-door evangelism program.

I was an extremely good evangelist. Those who accompanied me were moved by the passion of my delivery. Though we worked from a memorized script, I owned the words that I spoke. We walked around a neighborhood on the outskirts of Bouaké and prayed with the Africans who so willingly invited us onto their porches for a discussion about salvation. After "saving" people, I quizzed them to be sure that they understood that their salvation was based on the blood of Christ and nothing else. Then we turned them over to the local church and told them they needed to go there to learn more.

After a couple of months, I began to have serious doubts about the work. Was that prayer enough? What about the people who prayed the prayer but never went to church? What "saved" a person? I discussed these questions with the other participants in the Evangelism Explosion group. One friend said that she felt many people just prayed the prayer but never learned about Christianity. However, she felt secure knowing she had made an effort, and besides, we got to leave campus once a week. Another participant said with absolute conviction that she felt the work was about collecting souls for eternity. It didn't matter if they ever progressed beyond that infantile understanding of Christ; she had saved them from the fires of hell.

But I had trouble with the idea of collecting souls. It reminded me of two images of salvation I had seen in the anthropology course from Africa Orientation. The instructor had drawn two illustrations on the board. In one, God was at the center surrounded by several Xs representing souls. There was a circle around God, and some Xs were close to God inside the circle, others just barely in the circle, and the rest were outside the circle. In the second illustration, God was at the center, and arrows represented souls coming toward God from all directions. Some arrows pointed toward God and others pointed away. No circle separated the souls with God from the souls without. The class discussed the differences between the two models. Most of the class felt the circle model better represented Christian salvation as a moment in time, though they felt the arrows communicated something about spiritual growth.

But the model with the arrows intrigued me far more than the circle model. I loved the freedom and fluidity of it. The practice of seeing cultural differences had made me appreciate how drastically people can change. I had felt myself change as I learned French and adapted to French culture, and now I was learning a new way of thinking and being from living in Africa. It made sense to me that maybe we changed a lot in our relationship with God, moving like the arrows instead of staying still, like the Xs. How could I define a "moment" of salvation when I had personally experienced such drastic changes in how I understood God?

I also began to question our evangelizing methods. Wasn't I sort of scaring people into belief? I had been taught that the most important thing about salvation is that we can't *work* for it. It came freely. So wasn't my feeling that they needed more knowledge as a Christian a different way of asking someone to "earn" salvation? And if grace comes so freely, why would God decide so flippantly between someone who had heard my message and someone who hadn't. How could something as simple as hearing be the dividing line between heaven and hell?

I left Evangelism Explosion after only a year in the program and began to take a more cynical, defensive posture toward the Christian leaders at my school. Yet I stayed and completed my three years of high school in Bouaké. I still belonged with those students. That security was more powerful than any criticisms I had of the school. And I still basically believed in the same God, it was just getting more confusing.

I witnessed the way that Christian doctrines ran up against African culture in unpleasant ways. My boyfriend during my senior year belonged to the Freewill Baptist Mission. He told me one day that his father and the other male missionaries were having troubles with men who had converted to Christianity after marrying multiple wives and now wanted to be church leaders. It wasn't "biblical" to al-low this. So the missionaries required that the men divorce all wives after the first wife. I was appalled by this arrangement.

"Where are these women supposed to go?" I demanded.

My boyfriend got irritated with me for asking this question.

"It's not an easy decision to make," he told me, "but that's what the Bible commands, and that's what my father and other men have decided has to happen."

I was surprised to realize that I really didn't care if the Bible commanded it or not. It felt wrong to punish these women who had no control over their circumstances. A girl in my dorm didn't wear makeup or earrings because her father told her the Bible said not to. I disagreed. Or I agreed that maybe Bible verses could be interpreted that way, but I didn't agree that this meant God didn't want me to wear earrings. So did I have to agree that God wanted these men to divorce their second wives? Was this what it took to be a Christian?

So many people throughout my childhood spoke with the authority of God and the certainty of knowing God's desires, but my observations only made me more skeptical. The mission field showed me the humanity of religion—the humanity of the people interpreting the Bible and embodying it as the world changed. I had come to accept the surrender of my life because I believed it was necessary for the salvation of the world, but all of these differing opinions and personal experiences left me perplexed about the God who demanded my sacrifice. Was it necessary? Could I still trust "my blessed Savior"? As the questions multiplied, I lost the faith I needed to surrender it all.

13

Jesus Wants
Me
for a
Comedian

by Audrey Molina

I Saran-wrapped my brother to a tree when he turned thirteen. My youth group made me do it. Not the devil, not rock music, not television. It was my youth group that had this impact on my impressionable young mind—you could say that Jesus was also guilty by association.

I didn't just wrap him to a tree in our backyard, or even our front yard. Eric was attached to the Oak Tree. The Oak Tree deserves capitalization because it is old, big, and the centerpiece of our town. Everyone drives past it on their way anywhere else, and the long-standing tradition is to hang signs on the Tree to celebrate birthdays, weddings, and anniversaries.

Leave it to my youth leaders, Matt and Peter, to take it one step further. They were always good at that. The craziness was sanctioned because it had something to do with church. Earlier that fall, Matt and Peter had, with parental approval, pulled a popular senior out of his bed in the morning. Wearing trench coats and with pantyhose on their heads, they videotaped themselves as they Saran-wrapped him to the Oak Tree and left him there, blindfolded and immobile, as morning traffic cruised past. They showed us the tape at the following youth meeting, and warned that if you didn't attend youth group regularly, this would be your fate. We, of course, ate up the spectacle. It was half the reason we all showed up every week, just to see what could possibly happen next. When I was a freshman, Matt and Peter got mohawks because three hundred kids showed up to the first high school meeting of the year. The precedent was clearly set.

With this blueprint for mayhem in mind, I called up Eric's buddies and told them to show up at our house on the morning of his birthday. They rushed into his room and jumped on him. After this rude awakening, we threw him in the back of our family's ancient green Datsun station wagon. I drove them into town, and we met the girls from Eric's class in the Bob's Big Boy restaurant parking lot. We unceremoniously carried Eric to the tree, only dropping him once.

When the police cruiser pulled up next to the fifteen of us surrounding Eric, I could only point at the large sign we'd taped to his shirt that proclaimed, "Honk at me! It's my birthday!" to explain our actions. Apparently this was not a good reason to leave him there, between the banners that read "Ashley is 12!" and "Good luck on your retirement, Bob!" We returned to Bob's Big Boy for the breakfast buffet and headed off to school. It was just as well; I hadn't bought enough Saran wrap.

You could dismiss this as a one-time indiscretion. You would be wrong.

One of our annual youth group activities was Polaroid wars: a photo scavenger hunt throughout San Francisco. Teams earned points by running around the city and documenting crazy stunts on film. One task on the list called for us take photos standing ankle-, waist-, and neck-deep in the San Francisco Bay. Mind you, Polaroid wars happened in December, and you didn't have a chance of winning unless you took the plunge. We'd buy trash bags to wear as makeshift swimsuits—this being a respectable church outing—and hit the beach near Ghirardelli Square. We changed in the nearby public bathroom, and one of our chaperone leaders guarded our clothes. Wrapped only in a thin layer of plastic, we'd yell and dance around barefoot on the cold sand before we rushed into the frigid water. Tourists loved us. They probably thought this happened every day.

• • •

The popular girls at school invited me to youth group in the seventh grade. I didn't know what they were talking about, but when the popular girls invite you somewhere, you go. When I walked into the gym, the popular girls immediately ditched me, having fulfilled their evangelistic quota for the week. There was a huge game of dodge ball in progress.

Until that point, my understanding of God came from going to Catholic Mass and attending Bible class at my nondenominational Christian private school. These hadn't been the most ideal situations for me to cultivate a deep spirituality. My family went to Mass every Sunday. I was expected to sit still during church and be silent. Sitting still wouldn't have been a problem except the church was always frigid—how else was I supposed to stay warm? And being quiet wouldn't have been a problem either, except I was unbelievably bored. Sometimes I'd sneak a library book in with me, but my mom always took it away. I'd use my baby brother David as an excuse to take him outside, claiming he was restless even though he showed no signs of this. That hour on Sunday was the longest one of the whole week, and there was nothing I could do to make it feel shorter.

My parents made me attend catechism classes after school in preparation for my First Communion. As far as I can recall, these classes mostly involved us being unholy terrors, running around and hiding under desks. Before Communion, we had to go to confession. But no one said anything about how confession violated two childhood commandments: don't ever go in the closet and shut the door after you, and don't talk to strangers.

Bible class at school was more of the same. Each week, we memorized Scripture passages and the books of the Bible. Then we took our turns at the teacher's desk quickly mumbling the hard-to-pronounce words in the right order before we forgot them five minutes later.

Naturally, I thought God was kind of boring. He was as cold as the church he lived in. The gospel was just another thing I had to know, like all the states and their capitals. So the sight of people at this youth group running around, yelling, and laughing as they played games in the church gym flabbergasted me. I could not comprehend what this had to do with church or with God—people were actually having *fun*. I was appalled. I was overwhelmed. I was completely hooked. It was like running away and joining the circus.

As it turns out, the most rebellious thing I did as a teenager was to become a Presbyterian. Filipinos are Catholic like Italians are Catholic. I didn't realize how much I was shaking the family tree until the Christmas after I became a member of the church. One of my aunts had this funny look on her face when she referred to me as "the Presbyterian."

Of course, I paid little heed to this. God was more *real* at youth group. God made more sense to me when adults who were not parents or teachers greeted me with a smile each week and engaged me in conversation than when I swallowed a dry Communion wafer or sat through a teacher's droning lesson. Being a teenager is like being in *Lord of the Flies*; the painted faces and spears and fire are optional. Discovering this youth group was like finding a haven in a terrible storm. I rarely missed any meeting or activity. I knew, without anyone having to tell me, that I was safe. The trouble with this, of course, is that once you graduate from high school, and you get too old for youth group, whatever faith you might have cultivated through all the good times can crumble easily. Being a Christian gets to be less fun, and, like a toy that's been outgrown, it falls to the wayside in favor of other things.

I can't really explain why that didn't happen to me, why I still call myself a Christian today. Maybe I had a strong moral compass, but I wouldn't presume to believe that. I suspect that the roots of my faith have something to do with a fateful night during my sophomore year. Paul had his Damascus road experience. I had this.

• • •

It was our annual winter retreat, and there was a talent show. The previous year, a senior had done his own stand-up routine for the talent show and had been a hit. As I laughed at his jokes, I thought, "Well, I could do that." In the month leading up to the retreat, I plagiarized jokes from the comedians I saw on cable TV. I bought a cassette tape of *Comic Relief 3*, featuring comedians like Robin Williams, Whoopi Goldberg, and Dennis Miller. A lot of their material was completely inappropriate for a church youth group audience. I told no one of my plans. I practiced in the secrecy of my room, with my Walkman headphones on, listening to uproarious audience laughter on the tape and visualizing how people would be entertained by my obvious wit. Now, I was a quiet kid who didn't say a whole lot at youth group or at school. There was nothing about me to suggest to anyone what I was about to do.

My name went up on the chalkboard, the fourth act for the night. I had neglected to come up with a catchy name for my routine. My idea of flair was wearing this garish striped poncho that, on my small frame, almost reached to the floor; I had bought it during a Mexico mission trip the previous year. I stood on the deck outside the door to the amphitheater-style meeting room in the cold forest air; I heard the rumble of the crowd. When I peered inside, stage lights blinded me, but I could make out silhouettes. I quickly realized that two hundred people is *a lot* of people. I didn't know a soul, at least, not very well. I quickly became drenched with the sweat of fear. It was too late to back out now; I heard my name called, walked out on stage to the microphone and began to stammer out my routine. The heat of everyone in the room fogged up my glasses.

I have blocked most of this trauma from my memory. The only joke I remember was cadged from comedian Steven Wright: "A cop pulled me over once when I ran a stop sign. He asked, 'Why didn't you stop back there?' I said, 'I don't believe everything I read.'" I messed up the delivery—it's hard to be deadpan when your voice is quavering. Things were not looking good. I could feel the audience's perplexity in the silence as my throat dried up. I was doomed; I was sinking like the Titanic.

Matt and Peter had dressed up as Phil Donahue and Ed McMahon to host the show. They'd made an applause sign to turn on throughout the evening to fire everyone up. I think they wanted to help me out by lighting the sign. Unfortunately, they'd turn it on just as I arrived at the punch line. While everyone whooped and hollered, I said the best part of the joke. Then we all stared at each other, each expecting the other to do something more. This happened at least four times. Timing is everything, you know.

As things rapidly spiraled out of control, I started yelling, partly in jest but mostly seriously, "Shut up!" as I worked through a joke. That cliché of a dream where you are at school, naked, and everyone is pointing and laughing? It was like that.

With dogged and unexplainable persistence, I finished my routine and sat down with a thud. I thought, "What have I done?" I remember how I wanted to crawl in a hole and never be seen again. I was sure I was going to be a social leper. I'd be assigned a weird title that odd kids have at school, like "Smelly Girl," or "Nose-picker Dude." One incident could define and dog you for the rest of your high school years. I would forever be known as "Lame Talent Show Girl." It would go on my permanent record.

Then something weird happened. The rest of the retreat, people that I'd never met before talked to me. They said I was brave for what I did, and they thought I was funny. I was perplexed. I thought I had completely bombed, crashed and burned in a spectacular way, which was true. I felt ridiculous. Yet everyone was willing to socialize with me. I felt famous. I made two hundred new friends that weekend. I could still hold my head up and not succumb to the paranoia that every snicker overheard was directed at me. Hearing kind words was like curling up in a pile of laundry, hot out of the dryer. This was my first encounter with grace, in all its unexpected glory.

• • •

You'd think that once I escaped adolescence, I wouldn't look back. Instead, I became a church youth worker, which planted me back squarely in the awkward wonder years. I had lofty aspirations of telling kids about Jesus and shepherding them through these years, just as my youth leaders had done for me. I remembered just how cool and wise the leaders seemed to be, and I would be just like them. I had no idea what a difficult job being a shepherd could be. I also underestimated the aptness of the metaphor of sheep for teenagers.

Spending time with kids outside of church, I found myself at a high school football game. Nobody except the players' parents actually pays attention to the game. The *real* spectator sport takes place by the concession stands. Small circles of kids huddle together, talking loudly. Even though they are standing together, no one actually makes eye contact with each other. Their eyes are always scanning the crowd, looking to see if there is anyone cooler they could attach themselves to. Social Darwinism at work—only the fittest will survive. This same principle had been at work when I was in high school and will be at work forever. There I stood with a bunch of freshmen, feeling uncomfortable with these old memories.

Someone told a joke. When I laughed, the gum I was chewing fell out of my mouth onto the ground. I paused, wondering if anyone had noticed. Of course, all the kids had seen and there was an awkward pause as they stared at me. How would I play it off? Had I still been a teenager, it would have been a social accident of enormous proportions. Seeing the stricken looks on their faces, I started laughing, and the kids followed suit. I realized that I was no longer beholden to the unspoken rules of high school social mores. It was liberating. It had taken me thirteen years to become a cool teenager. Too bad it was thirteen years after the fact.

On the whole, though, being a youth group leader wasn't so bad. They liked me. Of course, a teenager would never tell you that outright. Instead they'd clumsily tease me or try to trip me. It's the thought that counts, I suppose.

I gave as good as I got. Take for example Andrew, a shrimpy seventh grader. He sat behind me on the bus ride home from our ski trip. During the four-hour drive from Lake Tahoe, he would periodically poke me in the back of the head and snicker. I threatened him with retaliation, but he continued to dig his own grave. I bided my time until we arrived at the church. I recruited Kevin, a brawny high school senior to help me—most of the junior high kids were either eye-to-eye with me or taller. I grabbed the roll of duct tape out of my bag, while Kevin threw Andrew over his shoulder. We taped him to a signpost in the parking lot. We took pictures with him. Revenge is sweet.

Where else but at youth group could something this unexpected happen? I was first drawn to Jesus because of the fun—the dodge ball, the mohawks, and the crazy stories that only got crazier in the retelling. But I stayed, and I grew, because I discovered that if I made a fool of myself, people would still talk to me. I still wonder about that night sometimes. What if I had succeeded with my little comedy routine? What kind of person would I be then? Instead, the worst thing happened (on the scale of a teenage mind). Out of that failure, I emerged relatively unscathed, and it was because I felt safe and accepted.

It helped me to believe in Jesus, really believe that he existed and loved me. It is a story that is as unexpected as being suddenly grabbed and stuck with Saran wrap to a tree. You could have a simulated snowball fight with newspaper (this being California). You could dance like a fool, or you could say nothing at all. You could hear about a God that loves you and be loved by other people. And somehow, all of this made sense together.

God moves in mysterious ways.

A Woman Who
Fears the Lord

GENDER AND SEX

14

The
Slope

by Shari MacDonald Strong

> God created male and female, the male to call forth, to
> lead, initiate and rule, and the female to respond, follow,
> adapt, submit. . . . [W]oman was made to receive, to bear,
> to be acted upon, to complement, to nourish.
>
> —Elisabeth Elliot, *Let Me Be a Woman*

Of several early memories, one of mine is particularly clear: I'm
maybe four years old, admiring my reflection in the mirror on my
parents' closet door, thinking that God must be mighty pleased with
me. I don't believe that I am *more wonderful* than anyone else. But
as I eye my dark braids in the mirror, study my apple-round cheeks
and copper eyes—gratitude flooding my small chest—I strike myself
as being a damn fine piece of work. I ache with how deeply I love my
family, how desperately I want to do good in the world. Not quite
prideful, but more than comfortable in my skin, I know that I am
lucky to have been born who I am, in this time and place. I can do
anything, and I don't even feel guilty about it.

Not long after this, I start going to church.

• • •

The Sunday school teachers tell terrible, wild-sounding stories in
chipper voices. God turns Lot's wife to salt! God makes Abraham
think he has to sacrifice his son! God kills every person in the world,

except Noah and his family, with a flood! (Remember this, children, every time you see a rainbow . . .)

At my public school kindergarten, I am the type of student that teachers covet: an early reader. I stroll the halls like a young royal. The principal greets me by name; my work is adorned with shiny stars.

But at church, Sunday school throws me. I want people to think I'm smart, so I don't ask questions. The Sunday school teachers patiently explain that Lot's wife did something unforgivable, God was testing Abraham, Noah's neighbors were so wicked they had to die. They tell us that Eve caused the fall of Man, and that women are still being (rightly) punished, that God was so disgusted by humankind that he had to send his Son to die and wash us in The Blood so that we would be White as Snow.

I don't follow the logic. I'm disturbed by the idea that Jesus had to die for my sin—sin I had no choice but to commit, I'm told, because of the Original offense. Why would God destine me to hell for something that I can't help? And, anyway, "sin" seems like a pretty strong word, considering I've never done anything terribly bad.

"Your sin may not seem bad to you," the Sunday school teachers warn, "but it's sin just the same. Everybody sins. Even babies."

I wonder what a baby's sin looks like: selfishly crying for attention? *Spoiled little babies.* Then I wonder what happens to babies who die before they commit their first sin. What if I haven't yet done anything bad enough to classify as sin? I'm still pretty young. I think maybe I have a chance of squeaking in under the wire.

"No," the teachers say. "It's too late."

This strikes me as particularly unfair. I'm responsible for killing Jesus, all because of something I can't control. The fact that I'm a girl, like Eve, makes it even worse. Our Sunday school handouts make it clear who is to blame for The Fall. (Hint: not the pasty-skinned, Tarzanesque loincloth-wearer featured toward the front of my illustrated children's Bible.)

At five years old, I can't help but feel that the irreversible punishment for eating an apple—the introduction of death to humankind, brutal pain in childbirth throughout the timeline of human history, and the transformation of soft Garden earth into hard-packed soil—seems a rather harsh response to one woman's choice, made centuries ago. But without even a trace of sorrow or ambivalence, my Sunday school teachers—all women—present Eve as a foolish, easily deceived female, an empty-headed temptress seduced by the perfume of Knowledge.

I'm a bit enamored with Knowledge, myself. Given my obsession with the Bookmobile, I suspect that I'd have made the same choice as Eve. I can't help but see her as the story's protagonist.

Still, I accept that my interpretations are wrong. I believe what my teachers tell me, even though it all sounds crazy. I don't trust my gut, don't ask probing questions, don't wonder if they're reading the Bible as the writers intended, or as God would intend; I'm still a child—I don't know how to ask these things. I swallow what I'm spoon-fed. I'm a little girl. What else am I going to do?

• • •

By the time I reach high school, the Bible stories have long since ceased to shock me. I'm a good girl, completely out of touch with my sensuality and sexuality. Other kids listen to Queen and AC/DC; watch R-rated movies; dress like Jennifer Beals in *Flashdance*; hang out on Hood Street, smoking clove cigarettes and hand-rolled joints; flirt with each other in their parents' hot tubs; and drink keg beer from plastic cups. Alone at home, I listen to Keith Green and Amy Grant albums while sitting cross-legged on the blue shag carpet in my bedroom; I decorate my locker with "Bullfrogs and Butterflies— Both Been Born Again!" stickers from the Book 'n Bible. I'm the perky, innocent little sister to the boys in youth group. The boys all tell me that they'll "take out" any guy who breaks my heart, but it's already been broken by the fact that no high school boy has "taken me out" on a serious date.

It doesn't occur to me that this might be perfectly healthy; that I'll come into my own, in time; that there will be plenty of time for romance, and for sex, once I'm old enough to decide my terms; that it might be best to spend some time alone first, anyway, figuring out who I am before I bind my life to someone else's.

I've heard countless sermons telling me that "It is not good that man should be alone," that a woman's role is to help a man. But it's not like I have that choice yet, and I have no idea where I'll meet a future husband. During my sophomore year my dad announces in a twist of reverse snobbery: "No child of mine will *ever* go to college!"

I angle for my parents to send me to Multnomah School of the Bible instead, known unironically throughout the Pacific Northwest as "Multnomah School of the Brides." I tell them I could meet a nice Christian boy there. "And what I learn about the Bible," I say earnestly, "I'll use for the rest of my life!"

"Why don't you get a job in an office, like your sister?" my dad suggests. During my last year of high school, I sign up for shorthand and typing classes. I type 122 words per minute. I picture an unending future under fluorescent lights in a typing pool somewhere in the suburbs. I can almost feel the sky closing in.

I develop a huge crush on a sweet, basketball-playing blonde boy in my church youth group. I am flirted with, and I flirt back. It's a relief to finally be noticed, to begin to believe that I'm desirable after all. But when spring rolls around, Youth Group Jock doesn't ask me—decides not to ask anybody—to the Big Dance. I never do go to Prom.

When a boy from the 4-H club asks me out on a date, I find myself with my first official Boyfriend shortly before graduation. We have zero in common, but he tells me that I'm pretty and smart. He wants to touch me. Everyone seems relieved.

When The Boyfriend pushes the boundaries with me physically, I don't know how or where to draw the line. I had been instructed in youth group not to have sex, had been told that "petting" was wrong, but no one ever explained what that was. (I pictured a boy stroking my hair, like a horse's mane.) Like other spiritual dangers, intimacy between the sexes was compared to a slippery slope. There were vague warnings: hand-holding might lead to kissing, kissing to intimate touching, touching to sex. Having had little experience with dating, it all sounds theoretical and exotic to me. I'm afraid not to let The Boyfriend have his way, at least a little bit. I'm worried that he'll leave me, that no one else will want me. He says I've brought him back to God. But when I tell him "No" repeatedly, push his hands back, he doesn't listen.

"We need to stop before it's too late," I remind him one afternoon.

He looks at me, dumbfounded. "It *is* too late." I'm so dissociated, have been taught so little about sex, I don't even realized what's happened until he says the words. I have been floating on the ceiling, watching from a distance, and I know that what he says is true.

It takes me months to notice how badly I'm treated. The Boyfriend bosses me around, criticizes me in front of our friends. I can't even brown ground hamburger without him telling me I'm using the wrong utensil. One night, on a double date with our roommates, he flirts with the movie ticket-taker. When I confront him in the lobby, he turns on me: "Jesus Christ! Lighten up. Going out with you is like going out with a fucking stiff!"

As he and the others find seats, I wander into the darkness. They think I'm pouting at a nearby restaurant, but I walk more than four miles through the worst parts of town—pursued by cat calls, my body shaking on near-deserted streets—then drive to a friend's house for the night. The next day, The Boyfriend finds me and apologizes, promises he'll never do anything like that again. I know it isn't true, but I have to believe him because I'm not a virgin anymore. I have to make this work. Who else is ever going to want me?

A year after graduation, The Boyfriend wants me to agree to marry him. I know I have to say yes, but I can't bring myself to do it. I tell him I'll marry him someday, but that I want to go to school first. I apply to the University of Oregon, beg a thousand dollars from my grandmother for tuition, tell The Boyfriend I'll come home on weekends. We both know we're just pretending. He breaks up with me, jumps into bed with an acquaintance of mine, starts stealing from the company where my dad got him a job. I should be embarrassed, furious. And I am.

But mostly? I'm relieved.

• • •

At U of O, I meet the cutest boy I've ever known. Before long, I can count on two whole fingers the number of boys I've slept with. This is worse than having had sex with The Boyfriend, because College Guy is a Real Christian—the kind who listens to Christian heavy metal bands, calls God "the Lord," carries around a Bible, and uses words like "sin" and "the Enemy" in everyday conversation. He is also a virgin when we meet. I am Eve, the temptress, the Mother of Sin. Unlike with The Boyfriend, College Guy and I *both* feel ashamed. One thing remains the same: I don't use birth control. Planning ahead would indicate the *intent* to sin. I worry about getting pregnant, but somehow manage not to. The stress is nearly unbearable, but at least I can tell myself that *I mean to be good.*

• • •

"I want to spend the rest of my life making him happy, raising his family, enriching his life," I write in my journal, about College Guy.

It doesn't occur to me to pursue the goal of my own happiness. I don't wonder whether College Guy will enrich *my* life. I think of our theoretical future children as "his." None of this seems strange to me. My whole life, the church has prepped me to be a "helper."

At the end of two terms, we reach a turning point. College Guy's wealthy parents want him to move back home to California; they don't like him being so far away. I've run out of money for school. We decide that I will move to California, too, so we can see where our relationship is heading. The stakes are much higher now than they were with The Boyfriend. *I really need for this to work,* because I've slept with two different guys. No other good Christian guy is going to want me now. If this one leaves, I am screwed.

• • •

We convoy down to LA: College Guy in his hatchback, me in my baby blue Chevy Vega; all the money I have in the world—three hundred dollars— stuffed in the front pocket of my Levis. After a gas stop in Stockton, my car refuses to start up again and I spend a third of my worldly savings on a new starter. I'm scared, but also enjoying the adventure. The palm trees along the highway south leave me open-mouthed. I've never left Oregon, except the one time College Guy and I accidentally crossed over the Columbia River into

Vancouver and took a photo of ourselves in front of the "Welcome to Washington" sign.

The next day, College Guy listens at a restaurant pay phone as his mom informs him that plans have changed, that I can't stay with her in the city—or at their unoccupied houses in Laguna Niguel or Palm Springs, or even at their ranch up north. College Guy's father doesn't like the idea of their stands-to-inherit-millions son having a girlfriend. I call my parents, who panic on my behalf but can do little from six hundred miles away. College Guy calls an old girlfriend to see if I can stay with her for a few days. (I can't.) I try very hard not to let anyone see how humiliated I feel. I keep driving, not knowing where I'm going.

My car breaks down again in Inglewood. College Guy tries to leave me at a motel next to the gas station. The motel charges by the hour; the individual doors don't lock; the clerk at the front desk has to buzz us in, and there's no way to keep him from buzzing in anyone he pleases. There's a sign on the TV advertising the Playboy Channel, and mirrors on the ceiling; an orange polyester bedspread, and no phone with which to call 911.

"Don't turn off the light," College Guy warns. "Or the cockroaches will come out."

I'm afraid to touch anything. I crouch behind the door, crying and holding a piece of wood, like a weapon. I'm eighteen years old, and I've never been so alone, have never had to take care of myself before, not like this. College Guy turns back at the parking lot; relenting, he stays with me for a few more hours. Shortly after dawn he packs me into his car and delivers me to the house of my dad's elderly cousin, whom I've never met, before obediently going home to his mother.

• • •

I move in with my dad's cousin, Helen, at Leisure World, a retirement community in Laguna Beach. Her contract states that the non-elderly can stay for only two weeks. I get a job at the mall, selling shoes to old ladies, and spend my breaks folded into a phone booth with the Yellow Pages spread over my knees, dropping coins into the phone box, calling local churches. I'm certain my people will take care of their own. "Can you help me?" I ask. "Is there anywhere I can camp out until I find my own place? Someone's house? The church sanctuary?"

When I reach a live person, I get the feeling I've interrupted her lunch. "We don't do that," one church secretary tells me. "Have you tried the shelters?" suggests another. "Sorry," they say, then go back to their tuna fish sandwiches and half-typed newsletters. *Sorry, sorry, sorry.*

I scrape together my shoe store earnings and move out of Leisure World, into an apartment on Santa Gertrudes with three students from a nearby Christian college. The girls are rarely home, and when they are, ignore me entirely. I eat my Top Ramen by myself. College Guy and I talk on the phone in secret, make plans to go out for my birthday in June. But when the day comes, he shows up late, thrusts out a Hallmark card from the apartment hallway, and tells me he can't stay. I spend my nineteenth birthday alone, crying on my bare bedroom floor.

Unbelievably, it doesn't yet hit me that this relationship isn't going to work out. I can't afford to lose faith. In the months ahead, after we finally start seeing one another openly, College Guy will slap me, generally ignore me, and tell me he'll probably never get married—all while expecting me to cook his meals, to do his laundry, to pay for his long distance phone calls and, when he's not feeling too guilty about it, to have sex with him.

One afternoon, he'll total my car and refuse to report it to his insurance company (his rich parents will kill him if his rates go up), then go home to sleep in the house his parents bought him, leaving me with an undriveable heap for which Farmers Insurance will pay me eighty-nine dollars before towing it away. The accident will happen as College Guy and I are leaving an evangelical crusade, at which a husband-and-wife evangelist team will have just sweet-talked me out of my last ten dollars, with a week left to go in the month; I will have put the cash in the plate with a note bearing my name and address: "This is all the money I have. I'm hungry. Help. Please pray for me." A few weeks later, the evangelists will mail me a postcard, informing me that the Lord wants me to give more.

It isn't until after these things happen, and more, that a Quaker pastor will ask me, "Why on earth have you stayed in the church?" that I'll rise up and become angry, that I'll find the courage to leave— the boyfriend, the evangelical church. Then I'll experience the kind of hope described by Saint Augustine: "Hope has two beautiful daughters. Their names are Anger and Courage: Anger at the way things are, and Courage to see that they do not remain as they are."

It's hard to believe that it took me so long to get fed up, to begin to see clearly— until you consider what a therapist told me recently: the divorce rate within the church is statistically comparable to that outside the church, but when a Christian woman's husband is abusing her, she's far more likely than a non-Christian woman to stay.

I don't know exactly what finally pushed me over the edge during the summer of 1987, what made me decide I wasn't going to stay with College Guy anymore. I just know that one day, I was wondering if my boyfriend loved me; and the next day, I knew that he didn't.

• • •

Back home, I throw myself into the hard work of pursuing redemption. After walking away from College Guy, I feel a little thrill of self-respect. I'm not sure if any Christian guy will ever like me now, but for the first time in a long while, I am beginning to like myself.

I tell the youth pastor that I want to volunteer to work with the high schoolers. I want to throw myself into ministry, to love the kids, to help them avoid making the mistakes I made. I thank God for bringing me out of the hell that was my life in California, praise God for giving me a fresh start.

"What have you been doing with your life for the past few years?" the youth pastor asks me.

I tell him about dropping out of college, about following College Guy to LA. I admit that I slept with my boyfriend, explain that I've repented, say that I want to live a life that is glorifying to God.

The pastor shakes his head.

"I can't let you work with the high school kids," he tells me.

I blink at him. "Why?"

"I'm responsible for these kids," he says. "I can't have you corrupting them."

When I stop going to the church, no one notices. No one ever calls to ask what happened, or to find out where I've gone.

• • •

I'm twenty-five years old and still single when I land a job at a Christian publishing house. I still seem to draw guys who don't want to commit, but I've managed not to sleep with anyone else.

One day in the break room, the sales manager and his assistant notice me running out the door with my purse.

"Why don't you just bring your lunch?" They're heating up leftovers in the microwave—pot roast and potatoes, a harvest stew—complete meals prepared by the loving hands of their helpmeets.

"Oh, I'm not much of a cook." I shrug.

"Well, you'd better learn, if you want to get a husband!"

I stop at the door, rotate on one heel. "Any guy who gets me," I say levelly, "is going to *get more than a cook*." The words surprise even me. The sales guys exchange a look.

And then they laugh.

• • •

By the time I meet my future husband, at almost age thirty, I've been in therapy for a couple of years. Unlike the church "lay counselors" I've seen before, this one—also a Christian—is a trained psychotherapist. He is helping me come to terms with many things about my life, including the fact that I'm not a virgin. I still have a hard time believing that it won't be a deal-breaker for anyone worthwhile.

I haven't been dating Craig long when I break the news.

He takes my hand between both of his. "I'm sorry," he says. "It sounds like you've been through a lot." The look on his face is tender. He doesn't look like he's about to leave.

"You mean . . . you forgive me?"

Craig gives me a funny look. "What do you mean, 'forgive' you?" He grips my hand tighter. "It's nothing I need to forgive you for. It's your experience, not mine.

"Anyway, it isn't any of my business."

• • •

The first time I had sex with my husband was our wedding night. For a long time, I was proud of this fact. Later, I wondered if things might have gone more smoothly for us during the difficult, early months and years of our relationship, if we'd just allowed ourselves to be together. It's a moot point, since we'll never know.

Today, on the heels of our tenth wedding anniversary, I can finally see that sleeping together before marriage, or not, was never the most important issue. At the comparatively wise age of forty, it's hard for me to believe that the loss of my virginity was once such a great source of shame. That I let it keep me trapped in a downward relational spiral, for so long.

As newlyweds, my husband and I attended evangelical congregations. But after one pastor dis-fellowshipped us for challenging his from-the-pulpit shaming and manipulation of church members, we stopped attending church altogether. At least, for a while. I no longer call myself an evangelical. I'm not certain what I believe about atonement theories, about What or Who God is, about what happens after we die, anymore. I've become comfortable, even intimate, with uncertainty, with questions. With doubt. More often than not, these days my husband, children, and I attend a Quaker meeting, where we're encouraged to see the light of God in everyone, including ourselves. We listen for the voice of God within.

It's a voice that I've been hearing all along, though I didn't recognize it before. It's the same voice that told me, at four years old, that God was pleased with me, that I was a damn fine piece of work. It's the voice that urged me to break out of my bad relationships, that reminded me my worth had nothing to do with my domestic skills (or lack thereof), that assured me my future husband was right about his not needing to "forgive me" for how I've lived my life.

For years, I was warned by church leaders not to question doctrine, not to challenge the patriarchal order. I was told that doing these things would land me on a slippery slope. It turns out they were right. In my thirties, I did lose the faith I had in an angry, patriarchal, puppet-string-maneuvering God—just as they warned I would.

But I've discovered a new faith. A faith in a loving Other that is, inexplicably, simultaneously Out There Somewhere and also within. A faith that has room enough not only for me to believe in God, but for me also to believe in myself. The proverbial slope is, indeed, slippery. But the grass is soft, and it smells green and sweet. The roll down the hill is freeing. And as I lie here at the bottom, looking up at the clouds, for the first time in my life, I feel as if I have a clear view of heaven.

15

Feminist-in-
Waiting

by Kimberly George

When a personal Lord and Savior was offered me, I thought he sounded appealing for surviving junior high. It is not that I did not take my new faith seriously; it was just that other pressing matters were at play besides eternity. For one, youth group was an acceptable place to flirt with both Jesus and boys. And then at school, the Christian kids (though I was wary of their Jesus fashion accessories) did have the most hospitable table in the junior high cafeteria. They accepted anyone who sat down. The more popular girls at school were already establishing pecking order, and with my anti-gravity bangs and penny loafers, I was not exactly next in line for cool.

So at the age of thirteen, I came to Jesus to help me through the labyrinth of adolescence and the hallways of junior high. I was discovering the Bible, underwire bras, and Jane Austen novels all at the same time; I was sorting through pre-algebra, salvation, and shaving my legs. Right at the time I was wondering about spirituality, I was becoming more attentive to my sexuality, my own thoughts, and how I saw the world. When I was at my most vulnerable in coming to know who I was as a woman, I was searching out what it meant to be approved in a specific context. My femininity and my Christianity were inseparable. At thirteen, the question was not, what did it mean to be a Christian, but what did it mean to be a Christian woman?

And for the most part, the church was eager to answer this question. There is little self-discovery needed when we are given the blueprint. I remember an event that felt as if it was my orientation into Christian Womanhood—a women's tea put on by the youth group. A certain amount of secrecy surrounded the event: all I knew was that boys were not allowed and that we were going to be talking about how to get married.

Along with the other blossoming girls of the youth group, I filed into the home of one of our leaders, ready to receive the revelation. Tables were crowded with high-tea treats, our course in womanhood set to begin. Because I had squished my toes into a pair of my mother's high heels, I wobbled as I mingled about the room, curious to peruse all the faces and strawberries and scones and sugar cookies.

Plate arranged with satisfaction, I sat down and prepared for the lesson. An engaged couple—Bob and Annalee—were positioned near the front of the room, holding hands and smiling. She was a quiet and gentle woman, and he was a kind Christian man. In fact, he was probably one of the most gentle, humble men I have ever met, and they represented a very soothing picture of love. Their courtship had been quick, simple, and followed the formula I would be learning to arrive at Christian wedlock.

STEP ONE: LADY IN WAITING

First, we learned a key principle about our femininity: a proper lady does not show desire or interest, which would qualify as *initiating*. A Christian woman ought not to initiate. After all, Eve took the fateful bite of the apple first, and the cosmos fell.

"So she never called you, ever, not even once, to show her interest?" someone from the chorus of girls piped up.

"Right," Bob responded. "She never initiated with phone calls. She let me do that. And of course she let me plan every date." He looked at her adoringly. "Annalee had committed to being a lady in waiting." More adoring.

I thought of all my trespassing phone calls to boys with a wave of fear. I wondered if a girl can *ever* call a guy.

I asked my Bible study leader later. "Well, you never know when things could turn romantic," she explained. "It is good to start practicing your role in friendship, too."

Another hand went up. "What about showing the guy you are interested . . . you know, helping him out a bit?"

Bob explained. "Well, part of waiting is that you are committed to praying. And your silence as a woman is a very powerful thing . . . Paul talks about that. The man is listening to God, and your role is to respond to him."

I felt a bite of scone stick somewhere in my throat. I gazed at the trophy couple as they gazed at one another. This must work, I thought to myself. Who does not want to be adored like Annalee? And I knew Bob to be a good man. So why this tightening in my stomach?

STEP TWO: MODEST COVERINGS

Next we learned about wholesome Christian attire. "It is very important," Bob explained, "that you dress to help your brothers. Annalee always dresses modestly for our dates."

We nodded. This makes sense in principle. After all, we want to be respected. We want to respect our brothers. We had heard many times in discipleship group that it was important for our bodies not to be "stumbling blocks."

I noted that Annalee was wearing a billowing denim dress that stretched to her toes. She looked very sweet in it. I could not really detect her shape. I was not exactly sure what my body was doing in seventh grade, but I sensed that I ought to keep it all covered up. Nobody told me this, of course, but there was something in the unsaid that mixed with adolescent confusion; I started wondering if I needed a sheet to hide every siren curve.

STEP THREE: PASSION AND PURITY

Of course when Christians talk about dating, everyone wants to know *how far you can go*. This is the primary Christian dating question. We were a generation bred on Elisabeth Elliot's *Passion and Purity*, the standard guide to not kissing, even before Joshua Harris "kissed dating goodbye."

"Can you tell us how to make sure we are following biblical purity?" one girl chimed in, speaking to all our curiosity.

"Well, Annalee and I decided to not start holding hands until two weeks before engagement. I think this is a good timeline."

A room full of Christian girls nodded. We either had not thought about our sexuality or pretended like we had not. Purity sounded fairly simple, as we properly sipped our tea. I mentally compiled what I had heard spoken on the subject: sex is for marriage, handholding is permissible prior. Perhaps I missed something when I visited the ladies' room? My notes on the subject seem rather sparse.

FINAL STEP: MATRIMONY

Marriage, naturally, is the final goal to be attained. We learned that our ability to fulfill our role as a mother and homemaker is how we lived out the gospel as Christian women.

Bob explained: "Your submission to your husband is a great spiritual metaphor. As Jesus submits to God the Father, and the church submits to Jesus, so too the wife submits to her husband. It all works just as God ordered it."

Feeling a pang of doubt, I thought about my dreams for the future, which did not necessarily end in just being someone's wife. I felt the throbbing of my toes squished in pretty shoes that just didn't fit. Clearly, this was not me. But how could I refuse my role? If I refused it, I would have denied not only my femininity, but *God himself.*

I stared down into my teacup, before sipping the last cold drop.

I remember looking around the room, at floral printed skirts and dainty gloves and docility and wondering if I could detect another resister. While well-intentioned, these dictums about love and life seemed as plastic and arranged as the flowers on our tables. I wondered vaguely about my own desires that went unspoken. Was I alone in my confusion? Was there another doubter hiding behind her silence? If she existed, she pretended propriety as much as I did, sipping tea with practiced submission. Looking back to this scene in my life, I know now that my body held in its tension the response my mouth could not. I hadn't been taught the vocabulary to translate my visceral response to an honest voice. For me, the journey to find authentic expression was ironically born of what stuck that day in my throat—a lesson on faith and femininity that I could not digest.

I went through my teenage years schooled in teatimes, sermons, and Bible studies that taught me this version of Christian woman-hood. By the time I left home and youth group for a liberal arts college, I longed for space to explore my unanswered questions. Well-meaning souls in my church warned me against my choice of college. It was Christian, but not particularly the right kind. Another girl in my discipleship group was going to the right school; she went there to be a biology major and came home Christmas break major-ing in home economics. I, however, became a heretic, as one could have predicted.

Delving into both my faith and studies with honest passion, I took classes in religion alongside classes in English, history, and phi-losophy. My questions seemed to catch fire, lighting the path to my own Inquisition. One day, I barged into the office of my professor of Christian doctrine, dropped my backpack, and stood ready to make an announcement. The man before me, Telford Work, played the ide-al religion professor: he offered difficult questions to freshmen, and always had his office door open to debrief the disruption on young evangelical minds. "Telford," I began, a bit nervous about using his first name, and such an odd one at that. (Telford had insisted we use his first name.) "Telford," I tried again rather meekly, "I'm a *heretic*."

Silence. I thought I had delivered quite the blow. But Telford Work sat in his leather chair rather calmly, adjusting his red bowtie, and looking at me with a gentle mix of compassion and concern. I was waiting for heaven to rain down fire, but when nothing hap-pened, my emotion came in a landslide. Through tears, I began to ask questions in Telford's office that I had never felt safe asking with-in church walls. I had been learning from history books what it has meant for women's voices to go unheard. I had been learning why some of the suffering core to women's lives so often goes unnamed and unseen. And now, I was asking how the church was upholding age-old systems that silenced women and kept men in positions of power over them.

I opened the Bible and began to read prooftexts like allegations against this two-thousand-year-old institution: "I permit no woman to teach or to have authority over a man; she is to keep silent. For Adam was formed first, then Eve; and Adam was not deceived; but the woman was deceived and became a transgressor"; "[Man] is the image and reflection of God; but woman is the reflection of man . . . neither was man created for the sake of woman, but woman for the sake of man"; ". . . women should be silent in the churches. For they are not permitted to speak"; ". . . Just as the church is subject to Christ, so also wives ought to be, in everything, to their husbands."

Telford stayed quietly attentive during the trial. I put down the criminal book and continued my charge, somewhat floored by the fact that a man was listening, so engaged with my voice. I asked the question these texts begged: Why did it seem like this tale was being told by a man? What was I supposed to do with a sacred Word that seems to strip me of my own power to speak? How was I to sit meekly in a church tradition so aligned with patriarchy? I was speaking as a woman who read a sacred text of sixty-six books without one author of her gender, a text in which one woman causes the ruin of humanity with her curiosity and appetite, a text in which New Testament letters assign silence and submission as my proper role.

It was hard to be a woman and a Christian. And it still is.

I had learned to find my faith in the God of Abraham, Isaac, and Jacob, and I was wondering about the God of Tamar and Bathsheba, too. How was the Bible addressing the darker realities of woman's lives across the globe? Realities like domestic violence, rape, inadequate access to education, and poverty stemming from withheld opportunities. Life is not a tea party. The model of Christian femininity I had learned did not ask me to recognize or stand up for the necessity of strong, female voices in the church and the world.

Sitting in Telford's office, staring at the weightiness of Bibles and commentaries that lined the walls, I wondered about the implications of a god who was spoken of and represented in very male terms. Telford and I struggled together with Scripture. Together we opened the text and talked about the bloodshed that stained its pages, and whether or not the verses could be read differently. We talked about whether there was life in the words, hidden under centuries of patriarchal applications. The Bible paints a more complex portrait of gender relations than a few out-of-context words suggest. And yet, the difficult words are there. Who is this God? And how do I as a woman and a person, a Christian and a heretic, find myself in relationship with this God?

I remember looking up to Telford's face, wanting an answer. Instead he asked me a question, "Kimberly," he wanted to know, "are you still praying?" The question was full of possibility for me. Even if I did not trust that the church wanted my voice, did I believe in a God who wanted it?

When I left Telford's office that afternoon, exiting the Religious Studies building, I stumbled out into the light of the Santa Barbara afternoon and felt strangely free. Born again, even, like I had left a womb and my lungs felt the arrival of newfound breath. I had no certainty about the survival of my faith, as though for once certainty was not the primary agenda of faith. I had, though, heard my own voice, because of the presence of someone who was willing to honor it. It was a turning point.

• • •

After that, I continued to stumble into places of uncertainty. It was difficult to struggle well in the ambiguity; my well-trained evangelical mind wanted black-and-white categories. Was I a Christian or a heretic? Could I be a Christian and wrestle so much with the church and the Scriptural text? Could I be a Christian woman and pursue my dreams of speaking, writing, and leadership?

One evening, some time after my tearful confession in Telford's office, I was up late with caffeine and papers and tired eyes, searching Gospel pages. I don't even remember why I flipped to Matthew's resurrection story, but what I read awakened me. In perhaps the most pivotal scene in the Christian story, Jesus asked Mary Magdalene to preach the resurrection to his disciples. Mary wasn't exactly approved by the religious elite for the most important preaching in history, and I doubt she would she have fit in well at an evangelical tea party. Why would Jesus ask a woman to speak the truth to disbelieving men? It startles me that Jesus entrusted her voice to change history, and it astounds me that the male writers of the Gospels make this clear, even at the cost of exposing their own unbelief. It is a moment of Scripture pregnant with redemptive meaning for any woman who has wrestled in its pages. Jesus Christ gave the testimony of God to a woman who would not have been allowed to testify in a human courtroom. He commanded her to speak of what she saw and knew. Though her words were in danger of being dismissed, he still asked her to speak, and to speak without fear.

The resurrection scene is one of many moments when Christ praises the bold voice of a woman. I look in the Gospels and see Jesus doing the craziest things with the women in his life, from asking Mary Magdalene to go preach the resurrection to a crowd of unbelieving men, to praising a woman who unabashedly stormed into his dinner party to kiss his feet. I see Jesus being subversive to cultural, religious notions of appropriate femininity. Would the church ever teach a Christian woman to value such audacity and cultivate such a strong voice—even at the cost of challenging powerful religious figures?

I tell these stories, from tea parties to college epiphanies to the surprise of Mary Magdalene, because I believe there is much at stake in how the church is shaping "men to be men" and "women to be women." There has been a resurgence in evangelical circles, particularly in the backlash against the feminist movement, to set down very black-and-white models of so-called "Biblical Manhood and Womanhood," which do not do justice to the complexities of the biblical text. More often than not, "Biblical Womanhood" is a formula that does not consider enough the pressing need to develop women's voices. When I hear such formulas preached as though they are the gospel, my body tenses just like it did when I was thirteen, when I did not yet have the language to translate my own resistance.

I believe that our voices, when unspoken, will patiently live in our bodies, waiting for their birth, as we grow in longing for the more honest expressions of ourselves. Ironically, Christianity has been a midwife to my voice. Through the tension of faith and doubt and hope, I am learning to rewrite the script of an old tea party.

16

From Pro-
Life
to Pro-
Forgiveness

*Megan Kirschner**

We pulled into the church parking lot, which, ironically enough, served as the weekday parking area for the clinic. Evan reached over and put his hand on mine. His eyes searched my own, offering that look I'd seen several times over the past few months, the look that asked if I was sure, if I was ready.

No, I am not sure, I wanted to scream. *I'm not ready for this, but I don't know what other choice we have!* But I didn't scream. Instead I squeezed his hand and gave him that tight-lipped smile that let him know I'd be all right, that we'd get through this, the smile I'd nearly perfected over the past few weeks.

Evan and I had been engaged for several months when we first found out I was pregnant. We had the big traditional wedding already planned, with all the family and friends and frilly dresses. The church was already booked. It was the same church my sister had married in, the same church where my parents had married nearly twenty-five years earlier. It was important that these things happen as planned, if not so much to us as to everyone else. We were only four months from the wedding date, and Evan had signed a contract

---

* Names in this essay have been changed.

with a large company relocating us to Europe for a year after we got married.

I couldn't have a baby in Europe. I couldn't have a baby without any of my family around. I didn't think I could stay in the United States and let Evan go to Europe by himself. I certainly couldn't ask him not to go. I wish I could say these more logical, more rational thoughts were my initial reaction, but my first thought was that my parents were going to kill me. I was only nineteen, and I certainly wasn't supposed to be having sex before I was married. Twelve years of Christian school, years of church and Sunday school and youth group had taught me that much.

This wasn't fair. This was a huge and terrible mistake. I had cried when I first found out I was pregnant as Evan and I sat on the creaky, wooden porch swing outside his parents' house. Neither of us said much of anything. I struggled between the knowledge of my heart that I could not have a baby right now and the years of knowledge that had been forced into me by my parents' religion.

Verses from Proverbs reminded me that the shedding of innocent blood is one of the seven sins most detestable to God; even while the image of that sin growing evident beneath my wedding dress filled my mind. I remembered a verse from Corinthians that told me that my body is not my own, it is a temple of God, bought with a price. I heard the voice of my Bible teacher reminding us of a Psalm that said we are fearfully and wonderfully made. These thoughts tore at my heart, devastating, rampaging of their own will, and all I could feel inside was a creeping, calming cold.

We got out of the car, silently reaching for each other's hands as we looked toward the house across the street. More specifically, we looked at the growing group of people congregating angrily before it, spilling out from the sidewalk and into the street. It seemed their number had tripled since we drove by only a few moments ago.

We braced ourselves and pressed forward, stepping over the trash and leaf-littered gutter and crossing the street on a path directly angled toward the house. I heard the low chanting of the group as we neared, obviously excited by our approach. I felt my stomach sink inside my body. As we came to the outer edges of the group, Evan slid his arm around my shoulder. I looked down. I couldn't look into their faces. I couldn't look up at the images on the signs they were holding.

I knew the pictures on those signs without even looking, images of fetuses displaying fully formed fingers and toes, or adorable smiling children thanking their mothers for giving them life. I knew the signs because I had held such proclamations in my own hands, hands that now trembled as they clutched my jacket closer against my body. Not long ago I stood beside my family, beside friends from youth group, beside other families from our church, holding those signs in protest as we lined the sides of our town's main street.

I had been ashamed to do it, to stand out in public with hundreds of other people just like these. We stood ominously on sidewalks and grassy strips lining Center Street, declaring our beliefs with signs and chanting. No one smiled, no one looked at all happy to be there, no one made eye contact with those people passing by in their cars. Signs lined the streets, displaying pictures of fetuses and smiling children, Bible verses about children being a gift from God and murder being sin, all emphasized by the small, angry faces of those supporting them.

I hid as much as possible behind my sign, the quietest one available. In black letters on a white background it stated simply, "It's not a choice, it's a sin." I tried to disappear behind my faith. It wasn't that I didn't share the opinions of my fellow sign-holders on this choice of life, but I didn't share their strength; I didn't share their adamancy.

I knew that abortion was murder. I knew all the Bible verses that supported this belief. I knew that a fetus was a life from the moment it was brought into creation, not a soulless creature as so many claim. All these things I knew in my head, but sometimes the head is a long way from the heart. I stood with those people because I was a coward, I was afraid to tell my mother I didn't want to be there. I knew she would ask me why, and that was not a question I could answer.

I kept my eyes down, concentrating on the feel of Evan's arm solid around my shoulders as we passed the protestors. I tried to block out the images from their signs. The chanting turned to random, overlapping cries about this choice being a sin, that I was going to hell, that God would forgive me if I stopped now. I knew all this. I wanted to scream, but I knew I could never make them see life from this side of the line.

• • •

It seemed eternities after I'd returned a stack of filled-out paperwork to the receptionist before a woman with soft gray curls and librarian glasses perched on her straight nose appeared and called my name. Her voice echoed in the waiting room and I flinched, wishing again I'd given a different name. Hearing my name pronounced into the stillness made this too real, too permanent. I stood and turned toward the woman in the sweater and dress pants. The fine gold chain hanging from her glasses glinted in the light.

She glanced down at me over her spectacles, then at Evan, whom I was apparently reluctant to leave. "He can come, too. It's okay."

I breathed slight relief and Evan stood to follow me from the waiting room. We passed through the hall to another room, which had blue walls lined with shelved books. The woman motioned for us to have a seat at the circular table in the center of the room. She sat down and adjusted her glasses, properly crossing her legs.

"You're Megan?" I nodded. "And this is?" looking toward Evan.

"My fiancé, Evan," I told her.

"I'm Mary. I'm a licensed clinical psychologist and work Thursdays here at the clinic. I'm here just to talk to you both for a few moments before we take you downstairs."

"Okay."

"So you're . . . nineteen?" she asked, reading through my chart clipped to her board.

"Yes."

"And you're about eight weeks?"

I looked down, cold hands folded in my lap. I nodded yes.

"Have you been to see a doctor?"

"No," quietly.

"And this is your fiancé?" looking at Evan again.

"Yes." I smiled slightly and looked at Evan, whose eyes were focused on the clipboard in Mary's hand.

"When's the big day?" she asked, putting the board down on the table and really looking at us for the first time.

"Three months."

"Wonderful." She seemed to really mean it, too, and that eased me a little. "And you understand exactly what you're doing here today?"

I nodded, yes, yet again.

"You listed on your form that you're choosing to terminate so you can finish school? And because you're moving to Europe?" Her voice rose slightly on the last word.

Another nod.

"Europe? That sounds exciting." We smiled at each other, my smile more forced than hers appeared to be.

"Well, those are very sound reasons for being here today." Her voice was soft, reassuring. She was very good at what she did. She loved her work, and I could feel that. "Tell me, Megan, do you believe in God?"

That question hit me hard, made me swallow thickly against something I'd been fighting for control for weeks now. It was a certain, waking blow. "Yes," I replied, softly, shifting my fingers nervously.

"Good," Mary replied confidently. I looked up at her, surprised, and she smiled warmly at me. "And you've probably been told all your life that what you're about to do here today is a sin?"

I nodded again. She'd done this many times, and that realization both reassured and disturbed me.

"Then you've also been taught that God is a forgiving God, and that no matter what you choose to do in life he will love and forgive you?"

I swallowed again, choking on that lump trying to climb up from its place in my stomach. I looked down, my eyes burning and leaking a little at the edges.

The woman leaned closer to the table and continued in her soft speak. "Megan?" I looked up. "You're going to be okay. I promise."

I couldn't smile. I couldn't be reassuring, for myself or for Evan. I couldn't pretend to be sure of where I was and what I was about to do, as I had managed somewhat convincingly thus far. A tear traced along one cheek and Evan placed his hand, sweaty and firm, on mine. I felt the heat of his palm against my skin and fought the urge to pull away.

"You're a good person, and the fact that you're afraid of what's about to happen is a good sign. It's evident that Evan here loves you, and I'm sure you have a wonderful, supportive family at home whether or not you choose to tell them about all of this. You're not a bad person for doing this and you need to believe that God will forgive you," Mary continued.

I was not expecting this, not in the least. I felt ashamed, I felt somehow betrayed, but mostly I felt relieved. Mary had just said to me all the things I needed to hear but had no one to say. She told me all the things my heart needed to believe. We talked a little longer before Mary stopped to pray with us.

• • •

The room was cold and crowded with medical equipment and a hospital-style bed. I lay down as instructed. The nurse moved about the room, straightening, laying out equipment on a small tray. I turned to find her standing beside me, starting an IV in my left arm. I didn't feel it. I was too cold.

After a short time the doctor came in. He barely spoke to me. He pulled a machine up next to me, then put a small blanket across my legs and lifted the gown up above my waist. I looked into his very blue eyes, but he never looked back. I remember how black his hair was, that he reminded me of Elvis.

I looked up at the posters plastered haphazardly to the ceiling as he squirted cold jelly from a nondescript bottle onto my stomach. The doctor never bothered to tell me his name, never made an effort to explain his actions as most doctors are trained to do. He pulled an extension from the ultrasound machine, continued to make sure things were all right to proceed.

I closed my eyes. I didn't want to know what that great all-seeing eye would reveal. I wasn't sure I could. The doctor pushed the small handle of the ultrasound machine into my belly, moving, turning, adjusting. Finally his rooting stopped and he pushed just a little harder into my stomach. It was uncomfortable, but not painful. I tried not to consider the happiness that often accompanied such moments in medical facilities less ominous than this.

"There it is," he said, more to the nurse than to me. "Looks like about eight weeks." I swallowed. I kept my eyes closed tight but couldn't shut out the soft, spasmodic burst of heartbeat that echoed from the machine. That sound was life, that sound was something I never thought I'd hear and couldn't bear to acknowledge.

My heart sank. I let go of a hope I hadn't realized I'd been harboring, the whisper of a prayer that the drug store pregnancy test had been wrong, that this had all been one giant mistake. It *was* all a giant mistake, but not on the part of the little plastic tube with the condemning pink plus sign.

The doctor reattached the probe to the main machine and wiped the gel from my stomach with a Kleenex. My skin struggled between warm and cold where he had been working, the unforgiving air cooling the gel left on my flushed skin. I shivered.

The doctor stood and pushed his little stool to the end of my bed. My feet went up in stirrups as the doctor stood at the foot of my bed, looking at me for the first time, not really seeing, but at least focusing in my general direction.

"I'm going to insert this tube into your cervix, and it's going to work like a vacuum, sucking everything out through this hose. It's gonna hurt, but shouldn't take long."

I squeezed out his actions with heavy eyelids, attempting not to picture what the Elvis impersonator of a doctor was doing below me. He disappeared from the sight line of my blanket before I closed my eyes, and I tried to let him disappear from my mind altogether as the devouring machine groaned to life.

The pain tore into my body and tensed every muscle into a scream. But I didn't. I didn't make a sound. I remember the nurse asking if I was all right, and I didn't even answer. I tried to regulate my breathing. Deep breath in, long breath out through my nose like Mary said, releasing those ever blessed endorphins. It was hell, but it was short.

• • •

The recovery room floated. The departure of a girl near me exposed a large red stain soaked the tissue paper where she sat, the unforgiveable color of sin, her scarlet letter. It was the tale of the choice she had just made . . . the choice we all had just made. I couldn't focus on anything but that scarlet accusation from the semi-circle of chairs, the sinners of the round table of which I'd become a member. I quit trying. I closed my eyes and leaned my head back, letting the flow take over and relieve me of conscious thought. My body was shaking, trembling from pain and numbness.

• • •

I opened the door and was greeted by a sweet breeze. It sucked the sterile, doctoral smell from my nostrils and offered the promise of hope, the whisper of spring breaking the freeze. I walked slowly to the car, floating carefully in the pain, and opened the door. I tossed a brief glance up the sidewalk toward the front of the green house, my breath catching before I realized what I was looking for. The protesters with their condemning signs were long gone, and I was thankful that their emphatic beliefs had died down, as had the day.

Evan looked at me when I sat down. He wanted to ask, but he didn't. He wanted to know what had happened, how I was, and I was grateful he was unable to form the words. I closed my eyes and leaned my head back against the seat. I felt the car take off slowly as Evan steered us home. I wanted to tell him everything, but I didn't want him to know. There were no words for the last few hours. I told him simply it was one of the worst things I'd ever been through.

I tried to sleep most of the ride home, but my mind kept straining. I felt sick, I felt tired, but I did not feel guilty. I hated that. I had just committed what my head knew to be one of the seven most detestable sins, but my heart was quiet. I was afraid of what was wrong with me, what emptiness could allow a soul to feel nothing after such a trial. I tried to still that aching, gnawing voice by promising I'd feel guilty when the pain had subsided. When it all became real,

I'd be sick with remorse, able to confess this my terrible sin and beg God for forgiveness.

• • •

This was a promise never kept. Days turned to months. Evan and I married and moved to Europe. At times I would sift through the memories of that particular day, attempting to dredge up some guilt, some sort of remorse about what I had done. I prayed that guilt would consume me, allowing amends for what I had done. I prayed that when I chose to have my first child, the choices I had made would surface with the tides of regret and self-loathing I somehow longed for.

That day, too, has come and gone. I had my first child, a boy, beautiful and perfect. When they laid him covered in my life and still attached, breathing and miraculous on my chest, it was not regret that filled me. It was awe. It was incredulity. It was that instant, over-whelming love that every parent understands. It was in the power of that moment that I could understand the love that God has for us, complete with its undeserved unconditionality. It wasn't my guilt he expected. He had already forgiven me, his creation, the child he gave life to. That love was something I could not fathom until I held my own son in my arms. That understanding was something I could never make the holder of so many signs, the preachers in so many churches, or even my own mother ever understand.

Sunday mornings find me sitting next to my husband in a fa-miliar pew, my son downstairs in the nursery learning about Noah and Jonah, and singing the B-I-B-L-E. There is no guilt, no wonder-ing what I'd given up. There is an understanding and a thankful-ness for the power of that perfect love—the love I have for my son echoing God's perfect love for us. If the Sunday sermon happens to address the miracle of life, it is my son's face smiling up at me each night, after we've said our Now I Lay Me's and Love You's, that fills my heart. There is a peace in that understanding, that frightening and overwhelming love, which defines forgiveness more adequately than any Bible verse ever could.

17

Swimming
Lessons

by Victoria Moon

1980

To begin, I must confess one of my deepest, darkest secrets: I can't swim.

I can't pinpoint the exact reason for this handicap, but I have my suspicions. My mother told me that when I was very little, I nearly drowned, though I don't have any conscious memory of the incident. I do know I was raised in a strict, fundamentalist church, where no "mixed bathing" was allowed—no men and women swimming at the same time, together, in the same place. This, obviously, limited my access to water. I could not go to the ocean at all during the years we were at the church, and ditto for the local YMCA. My only chance to swim came when I was invited to swim in swimming pools closely monitored by the church leaders, and even then it was required that one dress modestly in the water, wearing clothes that covered you from the neck to the bottom of one's knee. I was always a rather slight girl, so the extra weight of the clothes made me sink like a stone in the water. The best I could do was slosh about, my legs heavy with the burden of the thick, wet material of my culottes. I can still feel the smothering, heavy fabric, still feel the frustration of trying to push myself through the water, holding on to the side of the pool with a death grip to keep from slipping under its depths.

Here is my first remembered attempt at learning to swim: the pastor of my church (who was also the head of the school I attended) had a several-acre estate in the country with an in-ground swimming pool. He decided there needed to be a physical education requirement for students at the school: we would all have to dive off the diving board of his pool into the deep end and remain afloat there for five minutes. This terrified me. I could not learn how to swim from reading a book. I could not answer questions about the depth of the pool or the different methods of swimming. I had to get into water over my head, and I had to swim.

When the day arrived, some of the older students were assigned to teach the little ones like me. One of the older girls, Beth, showed me how to pull the orange life jacket over my head and strap it in tight around my waist. I breathed a sigh of relief. Maybe this wouldn't be as hard as I feared.

"See? With this life jacket on you can't drown," Beth said cheerfully. She had an honest brown face and round, tinted glasses shading honest brown eyes. I believed her. Then she led me over to the side of the pool and, without a word of warning, picked me up in her arms and threw me into the middle of the deep end.

Water that burned like bleach filled my mouth, choking me before I could scream. I bobbed up to the surface almost immediately, but there was nothing beneath my feet, nothing to support me. I couldn't catch my breath, and flailed about wildly in the water, trying to gulp air as quickly as I could. I grasped desperately for the ledge of the pool, some solid thing to hold on to, but Beth pried my fingers away and pushed me back toward deep water.

"You'll never learn to swim if you hold on like that," she scolded. "Now kick your feet and scoop the water with your hands."

But my fear was stronger than her words, and I couldn't think clearly enough to do anything other than flail wildly in the deep end for what seemed like hours, crying and gasping, begging for help.

"If I take you out of there, you're going to fail P.E.," Beth warned.

"I don't care, I don't care," I sobbed, and she reached in and hauled me out of the pool.

"Just sit there quietly and wait until everyone's ready to go home," she said, and walked away, leaving me dripping and spitting water by the side of the pool.

Yet another memory of water: this story begins when I was ten, or maybe eleven, again in the pastor's pool. The sun is bright on the artificially blue water, the white pool liner dotted with squares and circles of sea green and turquoise. I am dressed in the regulation culottes, the weight of them heavy against my thighs. On top I wear a shapeless ivory T-shirt. But even with my legs, stomach, and hips— all dangerous aspects of my body—hidden beneath layers of clothes, somehow the truth of my sexuality seeps through, reeking, refusing to be sanitized or contained.

There is the bright sun, and bright blue water. And then a face, the frighteningly pale face of the pastor's wife, her hair black, her lips red, a holy Snow White. She towers above me, her lips razor-thin, a straight line in her tight face. My heart pounds, its movement showing through the sodden layer of my shirt as her eyes sweep my body, and I know something is terribly wrong. I run through sins I might have committed, but I can't think of anything that would cause her to be this angry. I feel her contempt burning me as her eyes focus on my flat chest showing through the wet tee-shirt, my nipples hard against the cold water and the ivory polyester.

"Get out of that pool and put some decent clothes on," she spits out, her eyes never moving from my chest. "You know better. And you are not allowed in the water for the rest of the afternoon."

I climb the pool ladder, dripping wet, so ashamed I feel sick. Suddenly I am a seductress, an exhibitionist. As I head into the locker room to change, I look down at my body, its narrow lengths and angles, my flat, bony chest. My skin is pale, my arms and legs thin and awkward, my shins dotted with a series of scrapes and bruises from some recent adventure. The only smells I detect are chlorine and warm sun on my skin, but it seems to me there must be another smell, too, a smell like rotten apples, oozing and sickly sweet. I cannot sense the odor myself, yet the pastor's wife smelled it as soon as she came near me. A woman's breasts cannot lie, and even before my breasts were formed, three years before the effects of puberty would biologically declare me a woman, I remember thinking somehow I must have already been a woman, a siren, a temptress.

I dress in dry culottes and a clean, thick, opaque T-shirt, and huddle beside the pool gate, waiting for the afternoon to be over. I determine from that day on to be invisible, modest to a fault, hiding my secret beneath the most shapeless clothes, the longest skirts. I would not let my sins, indelible as tattoos, be sensed by anyone but myself. That day, beside the pool, is the first time I believed I was truly Eve's daughter, full of the evil of sex, drowning in it.

2005

While searching the Internet the other day, I came upon an online Catholic encyclopedia and discovered Saint Walburga, the female patron saint of hydrophobia. Besides hydrophobia, she is also invoked for a rather motley collection of situations and calamities including coughs, dog bites, rabies, storms, sailors, good harvests, the city of Antwerp, and the plague. I am not Catholic, but there are days I wish I could be. Their faith seems so much more fun than the Protestant faith in some ways: lots of saints and miracles and fantastic explanations that the Protestants tossed out with indulgences and their sense of humor. Plus, if I were going to learn how to swim at the ridiculously old age of thirty-five, I needed something like a patron saint to get me through the process.

I kept searching the Internet for more on her, and found a site for an abbey, St. Walburga's, in Colorado. As I looked through their Web site, I found a place where people can write in prayer requests online, which are then printed off and hung on a bulletin board for the nuns to read and pray over. Feeling like an utter fool, my cheeks flaming red, I typed, "I am terrified of water, but I am a new mother, and I need to learn to swim, for my sake and my son's. Please pray for me that I may face my fears and learn to swim for the two of us."

I hit the "send" button. Hopefully, there are now nuns praying for me somewhere in Colorado.

Hey, I'm desperate. I'll take all the help I can get.

• • •

A few weeks later, I signed up for adult swimming lessons at the local YMCA. On the first night of class, I pulled on my bathing suit and looked at myself in the locker room mirror. Having a baby had taken its toll, and in the harsh fluorescent light of the room, it was painfully obvious. My stomach had this funny pooch to it, and my breasts, swollen from nursing, spilled out of the top of my suit in an alarming way. My butt sagged, and my legs were no longer shapely and thin. I had bought the suit long before I had gotten pregnant, and now I just looked like somebody's mother trying to be something she wasn't in a neon green bikini. I thought of putting a T-shirt on over the suit, but stopped short of doing so. It was too much like before, too much like the layers of clothes I had to wear as a child. I would not let myself be hampered this time. I would not let that be my excuse.

Shoving my feet into flip-flops, I grabbed my towel and set out for the pool.

As I pushed the steel door open, the humidity of the locker room immediately gave way to a frigid blast of air from the pool area. It was a big pool, filled with adults and children. I immediately noticed a young girl in an Olympic-style bathing suit and black bathing cap, pulling her way strongly through the water. When she reached the end of the lap lane, she did this graceful back flip underwater and pushed out in the opposite direction, her arms and legs moving in rhythm like a ballet dancer.

My heart sank. I was never going to be able to do that. I might as well go home. I was probably the only one who signed up for this stupid course anyway, and I was going to be down in the three-foot kiddies' pool with all the toddlers in their swim diapers and arm floats.

Then I looked over to the other side of the pool, and I noticed a clump of awkward-looking adults of various ages, shapes, and sizes, staring anywhere but at the water. Three were young African-Americans, a man and two women, and two more looked to be Indian or Pakistani women about my age. A white woman with blonde hair who had the comfortably used body of a young mother adjusted her towel more tightly around her. Another woman, a large, elderly woman with white, curly hair and pink, wrinkled skin, smiled absently in the way of an overly polite but desperately uncomfortable child.

These were my people. I went over to stand closer to them, and we smiled shyly at each other, uncertain strangers with a common goal.

A short, wiry man began walking toward us. His head was closely shaved, and his beard grizzled. He was dressed in long, tight swim trunks and looked about fifty. He was holding a clipboard and had a whistle on a red cord around his neck.

"Hey," he called out, "I'm Mac, and I'm the instructor for the adult beginning swim class." He began calling out our names, reading them off his clipboard.

"Victoria Moon?" he called out.

I hesitated for a moment.

"Here."

Once he had called roll, he faced us and smiled.

"Okay, first thing is getting into the pool," he told us. "And it's an important step. Just being willing to show up and do this is half the battle. So let's all get into the pool and start there. You can sit down and let yourself down that way, or you can go backwards down the ladder. Whatever makes you comfortable."

I sat on the edge of the pool and stuck my feet in, only to pull them back out just as quickly. The water was freezing.

"The water will seem cold," Mac told us, "but it will get better as you get in and start exercising your muscles in the water. When you are swimming, you use muscles that don't get used as much on land."

I took a deep breath and slid off the side of the pool wall. The cold water sloshed around my waist as I waded out closer to where Mac was standing in the center of the shallow end. Some of my other classmates, the elderly lady in particular, seemed to find even getting into the water difficult. Mac went over to help her, murmuring something encouraging in her ear as he gently eased her off the ladder into the water.

Once we were all assembled, he faced us.

"Number one, you need to get used to the water," he said. "I don't know what each of your skill levels are, but if you are comfortable, let's start bobbing up and down in the water to warm up."

Bobbing I could do, so I started moving up and down in the water like a discarded cork. Then I decided to show off a little, ducking my head beneath the water, coming up and shaking the excess water from my face and hair. The pool was a mineral pool, and the bleached-out chlorine smell I associated with pools was barely detectable. Instead, there was a taste of salt on my lips, the salty taste of the ocean.

"If you are comfortable putting your face in the water, that's great. If you can do that, try going over to the side of the pool, putting your face as much into the water as you can and, holding on to the side of the pool, kick out with your legs," Mac said.

He demonstrated the technique for us, and I put my face in the water, held on to the edge of the pool, and began kicking my legs as hard as I could. I kicked and kicked until my legs grew tired, and I stopped to take a rest. I looked over at Mac and saw he was still working with the elderly woman, talking to her and demonstrating how to dip her face into the water. She looked unhappy. Mac said something to her, patted her shoulder and left her clutching the side of the pool. I started practicing my kicks again, and Mac came over to gauge my progress.

"You're doing really well," he complimented, reaching over the water to grab a thin, blue board from a stack near the pool ladder. "If you're comfortable doing this, try the same technique, but holding on to one of these float boards."

I pushed off the bottom of the pool with my feet, holding my arms straight out and letting my body be carried forward by the blue float board and thought of the months of carrying Max around in my belly, all the months after his birth when my breasts were heavy with milk, my arms and back tired from the strain of carrying him everywhere we went. My body was rooted to his body, even now. Yet here in the water, I felt light, weightless, even if it was for a moment, and I liked how it felt.

Feeling courageous, I took a deep breath and slid beneath the water, pushing with my arms and feeling the waves bear me up, carry me forward. My chest grew tight with the effort of holding my breath, and I broke the surface of the water. Without realizing it, I had swum almost half a lap and was almost in the deep end of the pool. I went under again, this time letting my body drift down toward the bottom of the pool. I lifted my arms, and felt the water lift me up toward the surface. Always before I had experienced water as a dark enemy with claws, trying to pull me under and steal my breath. Now I tucked my arms and legs in close, and thought of my son, swimming for nine months in the warm ocean of my womb. *How odd we humans are,* I thought. *We live so long submerged, instinctive swimmers, and then so quickly adapt to life on land after our births. Even our biology seems to forget our origins.*

I came up for a huge gulp of air, then went under again, shutting my eyes tight, wanting to remember how it felt to have my life come from water, to feel safe there, to dream in fluid darkness and to smile.

The Voice of
One Crying in
the Wilderness

STORY AND IDENTITY

18

Inventing a
Testimony

by Melanie Springer Mock

Several months into my first year of college, I realized there was an optional worship service for students every Sunday evening and that anyone who wanted to be considered a Christian by her peers had better show up. For weeks, I had been blissfully deluded, spending my Sunday evenings running through the hills around town, then hanging out in the dorm lobby—a lobby which was, I'll admit, eerily empty, as if the rapture had come and carried away everyone except me. Students bursting through the lobby doors on those nights always provided certain relief: I had not missed the second coming after all.

Monday morning after Monday morning, my friends asked why I hadn't attended "Celebration," the student-contrived moniker given to these services. Their queries always seemed a bit weighted, as if my absence really *meant* something, either about me or about Celebration itself. Yet, oblivious to the gravity with which friends interrogated me about my weekend activities, I innocently persisted in my Sunday night rituals throughout the fall. Only when a friend suggested quite strongly that I accompany her to Celebration did its import become clear. Some were concerned my soul was in jeopardy, and only a weekly pilgrimage to the school's cafeteria—and to a night of singing praise hymns and giving testimonies—could save me. So, although I really wanted to be outside in the fall's waning warmth, I joined my friends.

That initial Celebration was my first real foray into evangelical-ism, although I was eighteen and had been a Christian virtually my entire life. Baptized at fourteen, my official entry into the kingdom, I had attended church with hyper-regularity throughout my youth; as the daughter of a Mennonite pastor, my life was rooted in the church. Sunday and Wednesday nights were consumed by church activities, and although I could always anticipate a rousing game of parking-lot Ghost in the Grave Yard before and after services, I grew tired of being the first kid to arrive at church events and the last one to leave. Sometimes my siblings and I were the only kids there. We were always at church, and church was always at home: Dad brought stories about parishioners to the kitchen table. We knew whose marriage was breaking up, who had moaned to my dad about hymn selection, and who was unhappy when a woman stepped into the pulpit. Indeed, the church was my life, even when we were not at church.

Yet despite my immersion in a Christian culture, I knew very little about evangelical Christians. I had heard rumors about fren-zied worship services and about tongue-speaking parishioners who danced in church aisles. Those services seemed so far removed from my own church that I could hardly believe such Christians existed. After all, our church unfailingly followed a prescribed pattern—not so scripted as the Catholics, certainly, but scripted nonetheless. We knew what to expect in each Sunday's service, down to the familiar brightly colored bulletins. The only variation, in worship leaders, was really no variation at all. If Don led worship, we would sing familiar songs to a autoharp; if Steve led, we would stumble through hymns no one knew; if Lois, half the congregation would sing tight-lipped, as they believed women were not supposed to lead worship. Because Mennonites were so predictable—nothing seemed different, even when we attended other Mennonite congregations—evangelicals ap-peared wild by comparison, even unreal, an image manufactured by made-for-television movies, akin to the crazy religious zealots who bit heads off snakes and stole money from poor widows.

That I chose to attend an evangelical Christian school, George Fox College, concerned my parents a little; they were hoping I would attend the safe familiarity of a Mennonite institution, where I would receive no more indoctrination than my upbringing had already given me. Ostensibly a Quaker institution, less than 15 percent of George Fox College's student population were Quaker. Most students, including a good number of the Quakers, were evangelicals. Had the students been Quakers alone, the shared historic peace church status of Quakers and Mennonites might have seemed familiar and comfortable to me. But these were Evangelical Friends, more inclined to praise choruses and emotive sermons about personal walks with Jesus. Still, I didn't realize how different I was from the majority of the student body until my friend dragged me to Celebration. Up until that point, I had been going to chapel services several times a week, a college requirement. But these chapels were mostly staid affairs, where students sang half-heartedly, then studied while some speaker droned on about sanctification, justification, fornication— all new words I did not understand.

At Celebration, the worship took on a more fevered pitch than at chapel. Students swayed to the beat of a drum set, piano and bass guitar, raised their hands, and moved from chorus to chorus without a break; as one song ended, the band changed key and off they were again. Everyone apparently knew the words to each song by heart, but I dumbly sat by, unfamiliar with even the simplest refrains. Soon, the student chaplain implored worshippers to kneel and bow down to "truly praise the Lord," and most did, singing robustly as they planted their faces in the cafeteria carpet, home of smashed french fries and pot roast drippings.

After what seemed to me an interminable hour of singing, the second phase of Celebration began. At this point, students were invited to share their testimonies, their stories of an amazing grace that could uplift even the greatest of sinners. One student, an unlikely sophomore who always seemed a little dazed, perhaps stoned, began. His truly was a tale of woe: born into a broken home, his parents aimlessly adrift in despair, he spent his high school years drinking and partying and snorting coke. A serendipitous encounter with a youth pastor had saved him, however, and here he was, at college, looking forward to a life of ministry.

Another student stood to testify. Her story was a modification of the first; the same song, but in a different key. Her parents loved her, really they did, but they were swept up in their own upper-middle-class longing for acquisition and neighborhood popularity. She had gone to church regularly, was in fact president of her youth group, but drank heavily to medicate her middle-class malaise; she lost her virginity in a beer-soaked affair before coming clean with her parents. One twelve-step program and a Christian counselor later, she was here, at college, anticipating a future doing the Lord's work.

And so it went. Student after student arose to spin astounding stories of sin and decrepitude. The narratives turned on the axis of God's mercy, a mercy manifest through the kind ministrations of youth pastors, teachers, church leaders, and friends. Even the sincerest believers in my midst—those who led singing and Bible study and who always smiled broadly because of the Lord's good works—were branded by the stain of iniquity, by a boozy night on the town and salacious feels in their parents' Buick. Or so they suggested in their testimonies, often told with tear-stained faces but the same broad smiles.

I had never heard anything like this, not ever in my years of Mennonite church camp and Vacation Bible School and youth fellowship. For some reason, giving testimony had never been part of my Mennonite religious instruction, perhaps because testifying and altar calls were never emphasized among reserved twentieth-century Mennonites. At church camp, we never had tearful campfire "Kum Ba Yah" moments, no confessions, no altar calls, as seems the trend at evangelical camps; instead, we sang around a fire, then gathered for popcorn and homemade donuts in the mess hall. And at my home church, Sunday school classes were less about the emotional recollection of sins than about instilling Mennonite values of pacifism, simplicity, and humility. The Mennonite distinctive of humility surely compelled us *not* to testify: in doing so, we would be promoting our stories and ourselves over the good of the community.

Perhaps, too, my well-meaning elders who taught Sunday school and led youth groups assumed the lives of Mennonite youth followed a certain trajectory: born into the church, we would be baptized in the church, married in the church, and eulogized in the church. Straying into temptation—especially the most heinous kind, like drinking and dancing—was never much of an option. Given the intended path our lives were to take, the narratives we might tell would be hopelessly dull. Humble, but dull: "I was born to Mennonites, I went to church, I died." Of course, few of my Mennonite friends actually followed the patterned life intended for them; instead, they succumbed in their twenties to the haze of drugs and the burdens of unmarried pregnancies. If they had found God again, their testimonies would fit well among the evangelical brethren who testified in my college cafeteria.

The testimonies of these evangelicals filled me with guilt and fear: guilt, because my life had been so serene by comparison, and fear, because my life had been so serene by comparison. After all, I was certain I would have to impart my narrative to the masses, too, and I had no lurid sins to which I could confess, only run-of-the-mill transgressions like envy and sloth. I could little imagine that my audience wanted to hear I had lusted after someone's hundred-dollar shoes or that I watched five hours of television each day. Somehow, being saved from the clutches of these sins paled in comparison to being rescued from the depths of promiscuity or chemical dependency. Given the nature of their testimonies, those depths were plumbed by everyone else at Celebration—and, for all I knew, everyone else at the school.

I was of two minds that night when I returned to my dorm after Celebration. First, I could forget that Celebration ever existed, fall back on my own Sunday rituals, and escape the threat of giving my testimony. In doing so, I would also prove to friends that I didn't care about my "Christian walk," as they liked to say. Second, I could become a Celebration regular, wait my turn to testify, appear the fool with my paltry sins, proving to friends that I had no deep faith, untried by sin as I had been. Evasion or acceptance: I believed myself a loser whatever path I took.

I chose evasion, which worked for a good long while, no matter how askance my friends looked at me or how often I imagined they prayed for my soul. Evasion worked, I should say, until the coach of my track team suggested it would be nice (read: obligatory) to share our testimonies with teammates during our daily devotional time. The trap had been sprung, and I was stuck. I had to choose between giving testimony and giving up my beloved position on the track team as captain, and so losing the respect of a man whose attention

I craved, my coach. I made my choice. I would have to testify, the consequences be damned.

Already an astute student of literature, though: I knew my testimony, my narrative, had to contain a certain level of excitement to captivate my audience. After hearing my peers' testimonies at Celebration, I also knew exactly what constituted excitement: sin, and plenty of it, the tawdriest kind. I contemplated the construction of my narrative, its dramatic progression, the persona of its protagonist, its denouement. And I made a decision. If I couldn't conform the conventions of the testimony to fit the relative blandness of my life, I needed to make my life fit the conventions of testimony.

Thus, when my turn finally came to testify, I made sure my life, and my transgressions, took on the darkest hue imaginable. The sips of beer my grandfather gave me in his garage were really a sign of my weakness for alcohol. The one time I went cruising against my parents' will signaled my utter and long-seated disregard for their authority. The puff of a cigar, shared as a celebration with friends, began my spiral into the seedy world of drugs. On and on I went, fabricating a tale of teenage rebellion based on half-truths and exaggerations. At the end of my story appeared the obligatory saint—in this case a high school running coach—who turned the tide of sin and led me to the promised land; this was a nice touch to my story, I knew my audience, composed of runners, would especially appreciate this type of savior. And my audience, I could tell, was rapt.

Of course, in my testimony I did not mention that I had immediately told my parents about the one drag on the cigar, nor that during my sole cruising adventure, I wore a seatbelt, got nauseous from gas fumes, and made my friend—driving her mom's Plymouth station wagon—take me home early. Nor did I discuss what I deep-down believed were the graver sins of my youth: the envy that rotted my soul and turned me against friends and family; the gossip that forked my tongue; the complete disregard I showed for peers who were uglier or poorer or stupider than I was. Nor did I reveal that my saint was an agnostic who did little more than express faith, not in God, but in my ability to be a good student and a good person, giving me confidence I never had and making me more a believer in myself than in God. Admitting these things, I knew, would weaken my testimony, would put limits on God's ability to heal the darkest of sinners. After all, it was easy to see how God could transform the envious; but to make a drunk sober—now sister, that took some powerful miracle working.

I had embellished most of the details about my life in testifying about God's role in that life; in essence, I had lied about my relationship to God, about its nuances and about the wonder of its eighteen-year evolution. Nonetheless, when I finished my testimony and fielded questions from my audience that day, I felt relief. More than relief, actually: I sensed that giving my testimony freed me from the burden of difference, of being unlike my evangelical peers in so many ways. I had at last been welcomed into their club, a fellow sojourner who had also felt the lick of flames before finding everlasting life. My testimony had allowed me to throw off the shackles of my staid Mennonite past, of the Sunday upon Sunday of church school and youth activities and potlucks that had made the story of my life, and of my faith, boring and predictable. Instead, I could become as the protagonist in my narrative: the wild child, high on beer and nicotine, cruising through town searching for fun, in need of Christ and remarkably transformed by the Messiah she had found. After my testimony, my female teammates hugged me tightly, grateful I had safely made a path through transgression to Jesus. A few male teammates—not prone to emotional display—clapped me on the back, thanked me for my story. My coach's side-hug, given as we walked outside for practice, signified that I had done well, in my testimony and in the life my testimony represented. I began that day's run feeling light, unburdened—a feeling that carried me through my workout and into my evening studies.

After that day, giving my testimony became easier. The worshippers at Celebration soon heard my story, as did members of my Bible study. While I never ornamented my narrative more than I already had, I never bothered to tell the real story, either; I had found a narrative that worked and felt no need to make major revisions one way or the other. That was my story, and I was sticking to it. On occasion, I was able to manufacture tears as I wove my tale, the clearest possible mark of my contrition—though manufacture may be too strong a word, for these tears were real, as was my contrition. Perhaps viscerally I knew I was a sinner hoping for God's mercy, even if my gravest sins were not the ones I detailed in my testimony.

In the years following my college graduation, as I found my way in the "secular" world and eased back into a fellowship among Mennonites, my testimony became rusty with disuse. No one called upon me to testify, nor did I feel a similar pressure to sacrifice my life's narrative for the scrutiny of others.

And now, more than a decade has passed since I last testified in any formal sense, though surely I've shared with friends the narrative of my past and of my faith's development. Without augmentation, this story no doubt lacks the verve of my earlier testimony. Sips of beer in my grandpa's garage were just that—sips of beer, given to me by a seventy-year-old man whose attention I savored. The cigar I smoked? If I mention this bit of my story at all, I admit that the cigar was a crazy stunt, that I felt sick after one puff, that my parents laughed when I confessed my transgression. With closer friends especially, I'm likely to divulge the more significant sins of my youth: the contemptuous relationship I had with siblings, fueled by my envy for my brother's scholastic success and for the easy way my sister drew friends—especially boys—around her; the snobbery with which I treated a family in our church whose kids, part of my youth group, were poor and ugly and out of sync with popular culture; the sullen demeanor I showed my family for years, so much did I resent being with them and away from friends. These, ultimately, are the iniquities that have stained me, continue to stain me, and from which I need to be saved.

Still, even talking with friends, I feel a tug toward the other testimony, the one that captivated my college peers, the one that privileges weaknesses of the flesh over those of the spirit. In some ways, I am much like a war veteran who only served stateside and never proved his mettle in battle but hides this from his home community. I worry that I have not yet proved my mettle as a Christian, so unremarkable are the sins that have whittled away my armor and have forced my trench salvation. The temptation to fictionalize my narrative would be especially strong were I called to testify in front of the evangelical students who now populate my classrooms. After all,

I know what my audience wants and what my audience expects from a testimony, and I fear that my real narrative might disappoint.

I cannot fault them their expectations, though; few want to hear a prosaic tale that lacks the essential ingredients of madness, mayhem, and then mercy. Perhaps that's the problem with testimonies: most people are compelled by compelling narrative. We don't want to read a book without conflict, a story without a turning point and a resolution. I also imagine Christians are drawn to stories that reveal a remarkable God who enacts miracles, not some wimpy God who gives people boring lives, lives unchallenged by the trials that will compel them to seek contrition, to seek God. Still, somehow, we need to privilege an alternative story as well: a narrative founded not on climax, conflict, and change, but on God's enduring mercy and love. For I believe God's powerful forgiveness extends not only to the gravest of sinners, but also to those of us who live, day by day, felled by routine transgression. Such mercy as this, extended to all, truly deserves its own kind of Celebration.

19

Why Isn't
God
like Eric
Clapton?

by Andrea Palpant Dilley

The sacred exists and is stronger than all our rebellions.
—CZESLAW MILOSZ

One winter afternoon when I was twelve years old, my father picked up a hitchhiker on the side of the road. My two brothers were sitting with me in the back seat of our slightly dented Plymouth Voyager van, which my grandfather had hauled off the junkyard and rebuilt. These were the cars we drove, junkyard orphans that had been rolled or flooded or wrecked. This one had a dent in the sliding door from a downhill tumble.

The hitchhiker was young, maybe seventeen years old, a tall Scandinavian-looking boy wearing light blue jeans with big ripped holes in the knees. It was thirty-five degrees out. He ducked his head low like tall people do, climbed into the van with us and then we drove off. The ensuing conversation—which I will never forget—went something like this:

> Dad: "These are my kids, Andrea, Ben, and Nate. My name's
> Sam. What's your name?"
> Hitchhiker: "Donovan."

Dad: "Oh, that's a good name." Pause. "Have you ever heard
of Amy Carmichael?"

Hitchhiker: "Um, no . . ."

Dad: "She was a Christian missionary to India who worked
to save young girls from sex-trade enslavement. The place
where she worked was called Dohnavur, which is kind of
close to your name. So you have a good name, a name
with Christian purpose."

Hitchhiker: "Oh."

I remember thinking, my father is out of his mind, preying on
this young hitchhiker who wanted a ride and instead got an exposi-
tion on the Christian missionary connotation of his name. I was
embarrassed in the same way I got embarrassed when my parents
said a prayer over dinner in a restaurant and the waiter brought the
ketchup while they were still praying. But then as we pulled over to
let the hitchhiker out, my father turned to my older brother who
was about the size and age of this boy we'd picked up and said, "Ben,
why don't you give him your jeans. It's cold out."

So my big brother Ben took off his pants. There in the back of
our Plymouth van on a midwinter afternoon, he peeled them off and
gave them to the hitchhiker while my little brother and I muffled
our laughter. Proverbial Christian wisdom says you give away the
coat off your back, not the pants off your backside. In exchange for
my brother's jeans, the hitchhiker handed over his own—the jeans
with big holes in the knees—and my brother wrestled them on. It
was a strange kind of redemption, a moment of goodness and blessing instigated by my father, my father the funny priest who blessed
a hitchhiker not with holy water but with jeans, his kid's jeans, given
over on a winter day.

But this I know only in retrospect. Then, in my early teens, my parents seemed painfully Christian. My mother was a friend of Elisabeth
Elliot, the woman-pope of Protestant evangelical Christianity who
said you shouldn't kiss before you're engaged. My father, an internal medicine doctor, prayed with his patients and talked about God
with hitchhikers and coworkers. Both my mother and father were
ex-hippies with very organic, soul-molding ideas about how to live.
Instead of a TV we had a flannel board that we hand-made with

all the *Pilgrim's Progress* characters cut out of paper, colored with crayons, and taped to the flannel panel: Mr. Great Heart, Obstinate, Pliable, and Mr. Worldly Wiseman. Instead of Superman cartoons, my mother read us big poster-book stories about Amy Carmichael who dyed her face brown with tea bags to blend in in India on her mission to save girls from sex bondage, and George Washington Carver, the African-American agriculturalist who changed America with the peanut.

These years later, I think I see what it was all about. I see my father who picks up hitchhikers and in that brief intersection with another human being says in so many words, "You matter, God matters, purpose matters," and I see my mother holding picture books at the dining room table, these funny little stories of hope and humanity.

I am thirty years old by now, out from under my parents' wide wing. My faith has been formed by their influence, yet it is also distinctly my own. I have spent a good deal of my life so far fighting Christianity, the church, and my parents with it; I haven't come easily to faith as some people are able to. But reckoning with the difficulties of God and life in the end defines what faith is all about. Garry Wills says in *Bare Ruined Choirs*, "The great enemy of believing is pretending to believe . . . the only way is the long way, through indirection, doubt and a faith that survives its own daily death." I have taken the long way, the way of doubt that paradoxically follows the truest form of faith: an impulse to shovel off the hardened surface, to dig down to the nutrient root, to satiate a hunger for deep meaning.

• • •

My struggle with faith in my late teens and early twenties was enigmatic for many reasons, one of which was the fact that I had had a healthy childhood in a healthy church. I grew up in Spokane, Washington in an old Presbyterian church called Knox, built in 1888, burned down in a fire at the turn of the century, and rebuilt in the early 1900s. It was jammed into a low-income neighborhood in the middle of the city, but we liked it like that—shabby and urban, rough and unrefined, beautiful in the way that back alleys can be beautiful.

Our youth pastor was a tall, lean man named Van who wore a leather jacket and rode a motorcycle. We thought he was the coolest thing since push-up popsicles, a pastor who sped around on a two-wheeler, pulled into the pastor's parking spot, and took off his helmet and jacket like Tom Cruise in *Top Gun*. Van had a vision for the neighborhood—he did what most churches forget to do, which is get to know the people next door. Every week Van played hoops with the high school guys from the neighborhood, all these tall scruffy boys who came from small scruffy houses to play hoops with the youth pastor in our basement gym. They loved him for it, and we loved him for being loved by the neighborhood rough-ups who competed in the church league and called themselves "Hard Knox."

The church had a top-notch internship program that drew college kids from all over the West Coast to work with our church youth every summer. They were icons the way Van was an icon on his motorcycle, all these cool college kids who came to hang out with us all summer long. They took us to camp. They taught youth group. They led VBS. For VBS one year, all the college interns dressed up in superhero costumes, pop culture icons appropriated for Jesus: Batman and Robin, Wonder Woman, and Spiderman. Spiderman stole the show one morning in the sanctuary, leaping off the balcony in his blue leotard in a staged skit that went wrong when his costume snagged on the balcony nail that was supposed to hold up the Christmas wreath every year. Somehow, he un-snagged his Spiderman leotard and then crashed into the center aisle surrounded by cheering children.

Flying Spiderman skits were only part of growing up in the church. We were young humanitarians in training, collecting cans for the local food bank, painting a church in a rural poor part of Washington State, and building a house in Mexico. This was one of the cornerstones of growing up in the church, being raised in a community that embodied Christian purpose and public service. It was an era of wholeness and simplicity, when life was all about mission trips and water balloons and beating up on your little brother. That is how I remember my youth at church: an image of innocence and amity and inviolable virtue, the swell of people singing "How Great

Thou Art" into the high wood beams of the sanctuary on Sunday with morning light warming through the stained glass windows.

I was raised by this church in a way, by good people who worked hard and lived well and took seriously the human experience as a long, drawn-out drive to integrate daily life with the wider mystery of life's origin and purpose. They were people who asked hard questions about what it meant to reckon with pain and grief, what it meant to believe in God, what it meant to love like Jesus in a sad and war-flogged world. They were people who taught me Sunday school and gave me my first Bible and came to my birthday party.

But love is never enough. Nothing is ever enough, when you tip over the steep edge from age twelve to thirteen and plummet into puberty. This is when you grow big feet and everything about you becomes awkward, including your heart. The world is not enough. My Sunday school teachers can tell you what happened to me when I hit puberty. I started asking mean questions—questions I knew they couldn't answer easily, questions that people had been wrestling with in more sophisticated forms for centuries. I sat on a ratty old avocado-colored couch in the youth group room every Sunday morning and raised my skinny arm to demand all sorts of impossible answers to impossible questions. I asked questions until one of my brother's friends told me to stop asking *so many questions*, emphasis on *many*. But I wanted to know:

> Why is there a sad homeless man standing on the corner in the cold?
>
> If God is real, why don't my friends at school know about it?
>
> Why doesn't God talk like he talked to Moses? Why doesn't God burn in bushes?
>
> Why is there so much war in the Old Testament?
>
> Why did Jesus show up with a body just once in all of history?

When I was in seventh-grade English, my teacher required us each to bring our own book for free reading time at the beginning of class. I brought to school with me one day a book that resembled in shape and size the small, cheap, paperback novels you find stuffed in the back shelves of used bookstores. It had a simple cover with a title printed boldly in the middle: *Disappointment with God* by Philip

Yancey. I remember my teacher leaning over my desk with her eye-brow raised at a book that no doubt seemed like a precocious choice for a thirteen-year-old, but at the time it seemed like a perfectly natural book for me to read. How else do you talk about faith but in terms of doubt and disappointment?

I was undergoing what psychologists so conspicuously call "individuation," trying to sift through every characteristic of identity formation as a teenager: my self, my church, my family, my history, and mostly my faith. And yet somehow in the midst of growing skepticism, my questions paradoxically drove me to find company with people of deep faith, a buffer zone of more seasoned belief. Poet Annie Dwyer writes in "Exodus": "I surround myself with belief, / The way the blind surround themselves / With those who can see." I was flanked on all sides by a community of people with integrity and intelligence who believed in the love of God and the weight of goodness. My father was one of them.

When I was at the height of my teenage years I started fighting with my dad, not over the usual curfews and chores, although we had those fights, too, but over theology and metaphysics and church. It was the kind of fighting that is robust and important, the kind of fighting that every kid should have if they need it. My dad and I would sit on the couch in our living room and duke it out; I did most of the railing, and he did most of the reasoned responding, but we both had fire to burn. It drove my mother nuts—she used to leave the room, tired of listening to her daughter's drawn-out exhibition of anger and skepticism.

When I came home from the dentist one day I wanted to know, *why did God make us with teeth that deteriorate, when half the world doesn't have the means to fix them? What does that say about God?* There was a whole litany of correlated questions on a variety of theological issues. One question in particular was precipitated by a funny sort of experience that I had with my dad when I was seventeen years old.

On a Saturday morning only a few months before I went off to college, I drove with my dad on an errand up to a hi-fi technology store ten minutes from home to pick up speakers for my desktop computer. He started wandering around in one direction and I started wandering around in another direction until I came across a TV playing a concert of Eric Clapton live and "unplugged."

I love Eric Clapton. He has a laid-back lilt in his voice, an air of coolness and grit when he leans over his guitar with a cigarette and strokes the strings for sound. I don't remember which song he was playing in that piece of the concert, maybe "Running on Faith" or "Malted Milk," but what mattered was the ethos: I watched his audience swaying with the unmistakable demeanor of worship that comes with the experience of good music.

I know now what that attitude of worship means. I listen to music as prophecy. As memory. As orchestrated longing. It feeds the hunger inside but also extends it; no music is ever good enough or hard enough or heavy enough to leave you fully satisfied. But when it feeds, it feeds with unparalleled visceral power. And if visceral impact is the mark of greatness, then Clapton was better than God. He was a man, a man you could listen to and touch, a man wearing shoes and singing songs about grief and love and the San Francisco Bay.

It is strange to have an epiphany of spiritual doubt while standing in a hi-fi store surrounded by televisions, but that is what I had. I discovered what philosophers call the problem of the hiddenness of God—a problem that stems from the inaccessibility of God and manifests itself in doubt. So many of my questions were rooted in this one enigma: if God is real and loving, then why isn't God more present, more palpable, more communicative? In other words, why isn't God like Eric Clapton? Why doesn't God give concerts at the Met in New York City so that anybody who wants to can buy a ticket at the ticket booth and then go hear him say what he has to say? If things were up to me, God would have a rock band at Key Arena. Jesus would play drums, God would take lead guitar and vocals, and the Holy Spirit would sing backup vocals. Halfway through the second set, God would climb down into the mosh pit to dance with us, and then the crowd would erupt with whooping at this revelation of divine booty-shaking proximity.

But this isn't the way things work. Some people I know can talk about God like he's the guy next door you go bowling with on Saturdays or the lady down the street who lends you flour and eggs when you run out. But this has never been my experience of divine action and presence. It is much more removed, more obscured and veiled in the mysteries of life and earth. Some people would tell me the alternative is unattractive: I wouldn't want God walking around with a bullhorn. God in his providential protection of free will leaves us to our solitude. But when I was seventeen years old, solitude was overrated. I was dissatisfied with the whole setup. So when my dad walked up behind me in the hi-fi store I laid it on him.

"Dad, look at them. Look at all those people." My voice was agitated.

"What about them?"

"Look at how they're listening. They're looking for God at an Eric Clapton concert, and God is nowhere to be found. Why isn't God more accessible? Why isn't God like Eric Clapton?"

"Hmm," he said nodding his head with a look of pensive concern.

"How are we supposed to live with such *ambiguity*?"

"Well," my father said with his hands in his pockets, rocking back on his heels like he always did in a moment of thought, "You seek grace and truth and live in conviction of what you know, as best you can. It's all you can do."

His response carried weight with me. He understood my struggle with doubt more than anyone else in my life because he had gone through it himself.

In 1965 if you had been wandering across the campus of Penn State University, you might have witnessed an interaction between two students, one carrying an armful of biology books and the other carrying a handful of Christian tracts called *The Four Spiritual Laws*. My father was a premed student going through a "skeptic phase" as he called it. So when a student evangelist approached him on campus, my father pretended to disbelieve, playing the antagonistic agnostic, asking all sorts of difficult philosophical questions.

"I never did tell him I was a Christian," he told me. When we were kids, we loved this story in the same way that kids love their parents for the edgy, sexy stuff they did when they were young, like riding a motorcycle or smoking weed. It meant "dad was *bad*" back when "bad" meant "cool," just for giving some overeager Christian a hard time.

Even after my father married my mother—who is of stalwart faith—and they moved into a converted corncrib in the middle of Michigan in 1970, my father kept plowing his skeptic field, turning over soil in search of reasons. He read *Steppenwolf* and *Siddhartha* by Herman Hesse and *Cannery Row* by John Steinbeck. I picture my father in his early twenties, reading literature about the human condition, his long polyester-dressed legs propped up on a coffee table.

In the midst of my own questioning, I loved him for all this, I loved knowing that my father stood once where I stood then, gave doubt a fair shot and courted it with fairness and freedom to find the truth. "I wrestled with this stuff for a long time," he said to me once during one of our discussions. "And then I made a decision." But I was not there yet. I was still coming of age as they say, tipping slowly into adulthood and trying to find my moorings. I had questions that I dragged around like tin cans tied to my ankles, making lots of high-pitched racket on the road. I wanted God to hear me: "I would speak to the Almighty, and I desire to argue my case with God" (Job 13:3).

I was months away from graduating high school and going off to college, leaving home to strike out on my own and gather distance from the childhood that I loved, but like every childhood, healthy or cruel, left me partly unprepared for what was coming. I felt pangs of unease and a distrust in the doctrinal system I had been raised under. I distrusted the church for not having answers to my questions, for handing out superheroes in VBS instead of handing us the small hard stones of life, for not getting down at eye level to say, "This will all become quite difficult someday when you are older. Brace yourself. Prepare to fight."

I stood at the juncture between youth and adulthood, a crossing point that for most of us involves a lot of questioning and exploration. I had grown up in a good church. I had grown up in a good family. But still I felt plagued by doubt. What I am supposed to say next, if I follow the pre-scripted testimonial format for Christians who struggle with faith, is that *doubt* was the bad monkey on my back that I had to shake off with deliberate fervor. The script goes something like this:

Step 1: Grow up in an evangelical Christian church.

Step 2: Be exposed to doubt and the enticements of a secular worldview.

Step 3: Try drugs and cigarettes and Pearl Jam.

Step 4: Leave the church because of doubt and said secular enticements.

Step 5: Experience epiphany; realize vapidness of doubt and said secular worldview.

Step 6: Swear off doubt and return to church with penitent heart.

Step 7: Reestablish faith; discover good living.

But the truth is never that simple, at least for most of us. The best of doubt is what undergirds faith over a lifetime. Doubt is born from disappointment and disappointment is born from longing and longing is the mechanism of Imago Dei, the intention of God within us. C. S. Lewis says in his preface to *Pilgrim's Regress*, "The human soul was made to enjoy some object that is never fully given—nay, cannot even be imagined as given—in our present mode of subjective and spatio-temporal experience." If that is true, then this too is true: My doubt *was* my desire, to touch the untouchable, to possess the presence of God.

I am at core an Old Testament Christian: prone to Job's questions, David's psalmic longing, Cain's wandering, and Solomon's love of beauty and dominion. My faith has been predatory more than anything else, a hungry prowl in the dark and a practical, unrefined pursuit—like chasing a ten-foot tiger with a carrot peeler—something larger than life that has to be found with the inadequate tools of mundane life. I took the long way through a tumultuous time of doubt that started most acutely in my teenage years and continued into my twenties. What enabled my faith during that time was, paradoxically, simply allowing myself to doubt.

It *still* enables my faith. I take comfort in what the Southern writer Flannery O'Connor wrote to Alfred Corn in May of 1962:

I think that this experience you are having of losing your faith, or as you think, of having lost it, is an experience that in the long run belongs to faith . . . I don't know how the kind of faith required of a Christian living in the twentieth century can be at all if it is not grounded on this experience that you are having right now of unbelief. This may be the case always not just in the twentieth century. Peter said, "Lord, I believe. Help my unbelief." It is the most natural and most human and most agonizing prayer in the gospels, and I think it is the foundation prayer of faith.

If O'Connor is right, then my doubt is not a form of rebellion but rather a strong, catalytic longing, a desire to broach the distance between a finite human being and an infinite God, and my faith is a form of homesickness, a burden of desire that effectively defeats me in the fight and says to me, *There is more than what I see, more than what I know, more than what I am.* This is what the poet Czeslaw Milosz means when he says, "The sacred exists and is stronger than all our rebellions." It puts doubt and faith in perspective. They are two roots born from the same seed: a desire to dig down, to get my hands dirty, to reckon with the deep, subterranean truths of humanity's search for meaning. "Seek grace and truth," my father said to me, "and live in conviction of what you know."

I wonder sometimes what happened to the hitchhiker named Donovan who my dad picked up on the side of the road so many years ago. God knows what he thought of us. We dropped him off at the edge of an old cement bridge leading north into the prairie land of eastern Washington. He stepped out of the car wearing a donated pair of blue jeans, into the chill winter wind and a world big enough to get lost in but deep enough, somehow, to carry and sustain all our disbelief.

20

The
Journey
toward
Ordination

by Heather Baker Utley

"It's not a matter of *if* you're going to be ordained, Heather," Reverend Judy said, "It's a matter of *when*."

I was confused. I hadn't just asked Reverend Judy if I should pursue ordination, yet she was confident about my future. I had just told her I planned to move from Ohio to the Pacific Northwest to work with teenagers through a Christian youth ministry. In the midst of my explanation I mentioned, "Everyone seems to think this is just a stepping stone . . . like someday I'm going to be ordained." And then Judy nodded and smiled, like she (and apparently *everyone*) knew a secret I didn't—that someday I was going to roll over and realize God was calling me an ordained pastor.

When I say that *everyone* thought I was on the verge of ordination, I really do mean *everyone*. Before talking with Reverend Judy, I had met with several former pastors and members of my home church, and they all seemed to believe my jaunt in "parachurch youth ministry" was merely a warm-up to leading a church. Reverend Bill had gone so far as to conduct a full-blown inquisition to determine exactly why I'd chosen youth ministry over a pastorate. When I said, "I feel called to go the Northwest and work with teens there," he responded, "Heather, calling is not just about what you believe you're called to, it's about listening to the gifts that others call out in you. You should choose a job that reflects that, and you have the gifts to be a great pastor."

In the United Methodist tradition in which I grew up, there's no gray area about being a pastor. If you bear the title of minister, reverend, or pastor, it means that you have a master of divinity from a reputable seminary, you've been ordained by the Conference, and you've been appointed by the bishop to a pastoring role. Also, the odds are high that every four to seven years, the Conference is going to appoint you to a new position at a new church, just to keep things fresh. For many of the people who raised me, ordination was the only way to be in ministry.

But I rejected this line of thought—I knew I didn't have to be a Reverend to be a minister. As my pastors and loved ones assured me that ordination was the probable plan for my life, I would raise my eyebrows and shrug my shoulders. There's no clear reasoning why it wasn't what I wanted . . . it just wasn't. I couldn't share my reasoning with them because the only point I was clear on was, "Something about that violates me to the core."

• • •

When I was in high school, there was a very simple reason I never wanted to be a pastor: I wanted to get married someday. Most of the women pastors I knew were unmarried, therefore I concluded that for women, marriage and ordination must be mutually exclusive. It wasn't like there was a mandate that women pastors couldn't be married; I just hadn't seen many examples that proved otherwise.

Within a few years, my resistance towards the pastorate became less husband-driven and more denominationally driven. I became confused because the ceremonies and traditions that marked a United Methodist kid's progression of faith did not coincide with my own personal faith journey. As a requirement for confirmation, the junior high rite of passage in which I became an official member of the church, I had to meet with the pastor to talk about my faith. The meeting was a big deal—one of our many requirements on the checklist to becoming confirmed. Our confirmation class teacher prepped us for weeks, going over the questions the pastor would ask and teaching us the appropriate responses. The whole way through confirmation, my parents kept reinforcing that this was a big deal, so I definitely didn't want to disappoint them: I wanted to get the answers right.

On the afternoon of my meeting, mom dropped me off at the front door of the church. She looked so proud. I walked down the hall to Reverend Bill's office, and he greeted me cheerfully. I sat wide-eyed in his stuffed chair, scanning the rows of books, my feet swinging freely above the floor. He asked me to recite the Lord's Prayer and the Apostle's Creed for him, which I did impeccably. Then he started telling me about Jesus, explaining what it meant to put our faith in him. It wasn't anything I hadn't heard before, but I listened politely. After a few minutes of discourse, he paused, leaned forward, and asked the golden question.

"Heather," he said, "Do you accept Jesus Christ as your personal Savior?" He leaned back in his chair, all the while looking at me intently. I gulped in the silence; my feet stopped swinging. This was the part when it was my turn, when I gave the "right" answer. I was tempted to tell him the truth and say, "I don't even know what that means." But that wasn't the answer I was supposed to give if I wanted to stand up with my classmates on Confirmation Sunday, as the whole congregation beamed with pride to welcome its newest church members. I knew this wasn't the time to question anything.

"Yes," I responded in a sweet voice, "I believe in Jesus."

Reverend Bill flew out of his seat crying, "That's great, Heather!" He raised his arms in the air in triumph, like his team had just scored a touchdown in overtime or something. As he prayed with me and thanked God for my "yes," I grew pretty proud of myself, thinking about how this was going to make a lot of people happy. Yet I knew that I'd only said "yes" because it was the right answer and not because I really understood what I was saying. That small "yes," followed by Reverend Bill's exuberant response planted a seed of skepticism in my trust of the confirmation process.

The seed exploded into outright doubt a few months later. After Confirmation Sunday was long over and I had the certificate proving I was a real member of our church, I had an experience at church camp that changed my life. On our last night together, the counselors led one of those emotionally charged vespers services that often creep into camps and retreats. All of the counselors gathered the junior high kids into the dining hall, turned out the lights, and lit some candles. I sat along the back wall, close to my friends, and my favorite counselor, Mindy, read a story. I don't even remember what it was about, but I know I started crying. And my friends started crying, too. After she finished reading the story, Mindy talked to us about Jesus Christ in a way that made me feel alive and passionate. I prayed to God and said, "For the first time, I really believe that you're real, and I love you." In that moment, my heart swelled, and I was overwhelmed by the truth that Jesus was alive, real, and inside of me.

It's possible that my heart was touched more by a sentimental story than the actual hand of God. But when I got in the car to go home the next day I said, "Mom, Jesus is real! I mean, I knew it before, but now, it's like, I *know* it." She claimed I even looked different, that my face was lit up in a way that it had never been. That one experience was so powerful that over the next five years, I became immersed in leading our youth group. I even helped set the pace for the development of our church. My friends and I put together youth-led worship services, actively participated in Bible study, and recruited other students for trips and retreats. One time, I even rallied a few other teenagers to come with me to a church-wide capital campaign meeting where I spoke up for the church's need to allocate funding for the youth room. I felt I was becoming someone that others looked to and said, "Wow. She knows what she believes. She lives her life with conviction." And it was during this time, as a result of that one moment at camp, that the adults in my church and even the kids at school began asking me when I was going to become a pastor.

Whenever someone asked me about my future as a pastor, the hair would rise on the back of my neck, and I'd change the subject. I'd think about the conversation Mom and I had on the drive home from church camp, when I'd said to her, "Mom, it's weird . . . because confirmation class didn't mean anything, and this 'yes' means everything." Even though I was confident of my personal faith, the way it had developed made me skeptical of my church. I'd tricked an entire congregation into believing I'd said "yes" to Jesus in the pastor's office, but I hadn't really said "yes" to Jesus until two months later during the candlelit vespers service in the camp dining hall. I didn't have the heart to lead other kids through the rote ceremonies of confirmation. So while I had an immense amount of loyalty to Christ, I had no desire to pastor a church.

High school graduation became the perfect time to escape the United Methodist Church and find a spiritual home that was more supportive of the fluid, experiential faith that had changed my life. When I researched colleges, the evangelical institutions seemed like the best fit, so I picked one of those. The people there seemed passionate about their beliefs, because they talked about Jesus even when they weren't at church, and they brought their Bibles with them to church services and actually opened them. The evangelicals were also interested in mission work, which meant getting to travel overseas (pretty much one of my biggest life goals). The best part for me was that the evangelicals used guitars and drums during worship, which helped me to feel closer to God than I ever had by singing hymns to an organ accompaniment.

As I started talking to my new college friends, most of them were from churches I'd never heard of. One friend was from the Christian Reformed Church, one had grown up in the Middle East, and none of them really knew what it meant to be a United Methodist. The only friend who knew about the United Methodist Church said, "We left that church a few years ago because the pastor started preaching that homosexuality was okay." While I knew that the United Methodist Church was in continual dialogue about its stance on homosexuality, what I quickly learned at my evangelical college was that any church that debates whether homosexuals belong in church was labeled "liberal." I also discovered that I was the only student anyone knew of who'd grown up in a church with female pastors. This made women's ordination a characteristic of a "liberal" church as well. And in the evangelical circuit, it seemed that "liberal" was equated with "not very Christian." I was already disenchanted with the United Methodist Church because of my confirmation and camp experiences, so it was easy for me to accept that the United Methodist Church was "not very Christian" on most fronts.

Still, it was definitely difficult to believe that this was true for women in ministry as well.

I'd been listening to women preach or pray in front of congregations almost every Sunday for my whole life. In college, however, I'd hear a woman preach or pray once for every hundred times I heard a man preach or pray. This practice seemed to be based on the assumption at our university that women were not fit to lead churches. The biggest purporters of this assumption weren't even professors or preachers; they were my fellow students. Students would quote passages from Corinthians and Timothy that sounded so convincing that I began to question the validity of the teachings I'd heard from women pastors. I began reflecting on my experiences and saying, "Yeah, Reverend Bill's sermons were much better than Reverend Judy's . . . and she was always really limited in her ministry as a single woman . . . so it probably would have been better to have a man in her role instead."

This line of thought also led me to redefine my perspective on gender roles. Even though my own parents had raised me in a nontraditional, egalitarian household, I started to believe that God had created submissive women and domineering men. That didn't fit the model my parents had given me, where Mom worked fifty or sixty hours a week co-leading a family business with my dad, and Dad cooked dinner for the family five nights a week. According to evangelicalism, I'd been raised wrong or backward or "liberal." I couldn't remember a time when my parents hadn't been in accord and united and equal in their decision-making, but apparently, their model was wrong.

My acceptance of evangelicalism led me to reject a great deal of Methodist tradition, but the pressure of rejecting my definition of what it meant to be a woman was too much to handle. After nearly two years of chucking my Methodist tradition out the door to embrace the kind of faith that had changed my life, the glimmer of evangelicalism's newness began to wear off. I became extremely unhappy and cynical. I felt like the Heather I had been during my senior year of high school—fun, confident, and able to connect with potheads as easily as the senior pastor—had disappeared. I had become judgmental; I relied on proof texts to support arguments about spiritual minutiae, and I was finding it more and more difficult to relate to people who didn't agree with me. By spring break of my sophomore year, this pressure spiraled into a crisis. I broke down crying in a friend's lap on a missions trip to Honduras. (Please note that I cried in public on average, once every two or three years.) I realized that I'd let evangelical culture redefine everything I was. At that moment of complete breakdown, I said to God and myself, "I don't know who I am anymore, and I don't like the person I've become." Immediately, a clear voice in my head cut through all of the muddled, dissenting voices and said, "The only thing that matters is who you are in me."

I knew the source—I knew it wasn't just any voice in my head—it was God speaking to me. I knew it was God because the words carried a power that I did not have the energy or confidence to say it on my own. And I knew it was God because those words brought a peace and a comfort about who I was that I hadn't felt in years.

My identity wasn't supposed to be defined by a gender role or an occupation—it was supposed to be defined by God. Maybe I wanted to be a stay-at-home mom and use my pastoral gifts elsewhere, but if that was true, I wanted to make those decisions as a function of my own spiritual growth, not as a result of the church giving me a gender-based identity to become submissive and maternal. Gone were the roles, the traditions, the "liberal" way I was raised, and the "conservative" life I'd adopted. I felt empty without these pieces of my identity, but I was filled with hope. I knew I was going to start over—just God and me—and I was going to rediscover who I was defined only by my relationship with him.

It was like a weight I'd been carrying around for the last two years had been lifted, and I was once again the same smiling, glowing girl who had talked animatedly about Jesus with my mom on the whole way home from church camp. I knew that it wasn't about right or wrong religion, it was about loving God wholeheartedly and seeking out God's will for my life.

I had to start over. I had to examine my perspective on Christianity belief by belief. When it came time to tackle how I felt about women in ministry, I was nervous, because the perspectives I'd encountered were so conflicting. I knew that the scriptural prooftexts students had quoted to me were reflective of the culture in which they were written, and I also knew that the people whose faith I most respected seemed to accept of women in ministry.

As I looked to my own experience, I saw that the women who'd raised me and preached to me over the course of my life had loved well, taught well, and one of them in particular had shepherded both of my parents through the early stages of their Christian faith. There seemed to be little basis for not accepting that women could, in fact, be involved in any form of ministry. But still I was hesitant to believe that becoming a pastor was exactly what I wanted to do with my life. Just because women can be pastors didn't mean I had to be one.

During this time, I met a woman pastor who not only solidified my confidence in women in ministry, but instilled a desire to be in ministry myself—perhaps even ordained ministry. I met Dr. Marta Bennett, an amazing American missionary, during five months of soul-searching on a semester abroad in Kenya. As an ordained clergy in the Presbyterian Church (PCUSA), she taught graduate courses in biblical studies, training African pastors for ministry at a Christian university in Nairobi. But her ministry impact went far beyond her ministry role. She modeled Jesus's love for people in the way she cared for the people around her, sharing her living space with a young African couple in need of a home and being a benevolent hostess to a group of rag-tag American college students seeking free lodging. Also, she adopted two Kenyan AIDS orphans and proved to be an amazing mother. Apart from being unmarried, she embodied everything I wanted to become as an adult: an intelligent, educated, independent, well-traveled mother. She was changing the world by serving God wholeheartedly. While evangelical theology might have distrusted her ordination as a woman, I could not look at her life and question it, because I was in love with it. For the first time in my life, I saw an example of a woman whose ordination in ministry was allowing her to live a life I envied. For the first time, I saw that ordination could lead me to someplace more attractive to me than pastoring a dying United Methodist congregation; it could equip me to lead a life as amazing as Dr. Bennett's.

As I continue to grow up in the church and seek my own identity in Christ, my spirit is consistently conflicted. There is the side of me that sits opposite Reverend Judy, emphatically saying, "I don't want to be ordained," because I'm resisting the pressure that ordination means becoming a leader in a system with significant flaws. And there is the side of me that sits opposite Dr. Bennett, emphatically saying, "I want to serve God as wholeheartedly as you do, even if that means God's calling me to ordination." The revelation here is that at age twenty-eight, it's not yet time for me to choose the path of ordination, because I still can't sort through the opposing voices. I still don't know if I should continue serving in parachurch youth ministry, or if I'm ignoring God's call to pursue ordination.

At the same time, I understand enough about the theological perspectives in regards to women in ministry to be comfortable with God leading me to that place. After redefining my identity, I'm open to the idea that I could someday be Reverend Heather, as so many of the people who've raised me have always predicted I will be. But what I most desire is passion and growth in my day-to-day life with Christ. Ordination could be in my future, much to Reverend Judy's and Reverend Bill's delight, but when it happens, it will only happen as a necessary result of my daily pursuit of and obedience to Christ.

21

Spark

by Shauna Niequist

I loved going to church when I was little. Our church used to meet in a movie theater, and my Sunday school class was right by the candy counter, so it always smelled like popcorn, and we would press our faces up against the glass of the counter, looking at all the bright shiny candy boxes. It felt glamorous and exciting and busy, and there was something exhilarating and illicit about being in a movie theater when they weren't showing movies, like you were at an after-hours party. While I was in Sunday school, my parents were in Big Church. My dad gave the message and sang in the band, and my mom played the flute. When church was over, I'd run down the sloped theater aisle to find them on the stage, and I was very fast, especially because of the sloped floor.

I loved going to church until about halfway through high school, when I got tired of being a church girl, of being one of the only church girls in my group of friends at school, the only one on my pom squad, the only one at the party who never had to worry about taking a Breathalyzer. When I played powder-puff football, I missed the day we chose nicknames for our jerseys, and my friends chose mine for me. All their names were thinly veiled drinking references or allusions to scandalous dating experiences. When I picked up my jersey, it said, "Church Lady."

I knew they loved me and that they knew I was more than a *Saturday Night Live* sketch, but it hurt me. I didn't want to be that person anymore. I was tired of being different, and underneath that,

203

I wanted to know why it was worth being so different. I was different because that's the way I had grown up, and I needed to see if it was what I would have chosen on my own. I was starting to think that being a Christian, for me, was like being Italian or being short—something you're born into, that's out of your control, but something that will define your life. I wanted to see what I could do with my life on my own terms.

I went to Westmont College in Santa Barbara, two thousand miles from my town and my high school near Chicago. My decision to go there was partially out of heartbreak and desperation, having been rejected from my dream school, and partially out of a strange, deep feeling in my stomach that almost felt like hunger, a feeling I believe was God's urging. The great thing about a Christian college is that if you have some good old-fashioned rebelling to do, it's not that hard to be bad because there are so many rules. I had a tiny tattoo that I got in high school, and I got another one in Santa Barbara, a thin vine winding around my toe. I skipped chapel and pierced my nose and lived off campus and smoked cigarettes, and that's about all it took to be a bad girl. Another truly great thing about a college like Westmont is that there are lots of really good people, professors and fellow students alike, who will catch you when you fall down, and I fell down a lot.

During that season, all I could see about faith were the things that offended me, the things I couldn't connect with, the things that had embarrassed me in front of my friends. But even then, there was this tiny hope inside me, not like a flame, more like a lighter that's almost out of juice, misfiring, catching for just a second, this tiny hope that maybe there was a way of living this faith that I just hadn't found yet.

I thought about God, even though I didn't talk about him. It wasn't really about God, for me. I didn't have big questions on the nature of the Trinity or the end of the world. Essentially, I wanted to know if there was room in the Christian world for someone like me. Because it didn't always seem like there was.

The journey back toward faith came in flashes and moments and entirely through pain. I wanted to build my life on my own terms. I felt like having faith was like having training wheels on your bike, and I wanted to ride without those training wheels even if I fell. For a while, I loved it. I felt creative and smart and courageous.

And then everything unraveled over the course of a year. I had three best friends, and two of them went to Europe, and I fell in love with the third one, or more accurately, admitted to him that I'd loved him for years. I thought we'd get married. We talked about it, and we made plans, and we dreamed about our future. And then one day it was over. We screamed at each other in the driveway of my house in Montecito, my roommates trying unsuccessfully not to eavesdrop. He was, in his words, simply not ready for such a serious relationship. Oddly enough, soon after we broke up, he was ready for a very serious relationship with one of my friends. Ah.

I was heartbroken and confused and very much alone, and I started doing the craziest things. If you're a really sensible, stable person, and somebody breaks your heart, you might do something wild, like go out dancing and drinking all night, but that's what I did on normal days.

I dug out my Bible. I have no idea why, really. I sat alone on my bed on a Saturday afternoon with the light slanting through my window. I was a literature major, so my room was crammed with books, and underneath a tall stack of books on the windowsill, I found my Bible. I just held it. I don't think I even read it that day. I just held it on my lap with both hands, like it was a cat.

I joined a Bible study with some fine upstanding girls from my college. I'm sure they wondered what on earth I was doing there. I was wondering the same thing.

There was something inside me that was pushing me toward God, pushing me toward the church. And it was like learning to walk after an accident—my body recalling so much, feeling so familiar, but entirely new this time. I started going to church, but that didn't work right away, because when I went, I could still only hear the things that distanced me or the things that made me mad, the clichés and assumptions that had pushed me away in the first place.

I wanted to connect with God somehow, so I decided that I would go to the beach every night at sunset. It was the most sacred thing I could think to do. I wasn't ready yet for church, but I was ready for God, and I have always believed that the ocean is one of the surest places to find him. I sat on the wall at Biltmore Beach in Montecito and waited. I started praying a little bit more honestly and listening a little bit more closely. It was like seeing an old boyfriend, all shy and tentative, but really excited on the inside.

There was something inside me, some hopeful, small, faltering voice that said, "There's room for you." I don't know why, but I trusted that voice.

And against all odds, demonstrating that God is in fact very gracious and kind of a jokester, here I am, deeply, wholly committed to God and to his church. I tried as hard as I could to find a better way to live, to move past or through or beyond this tradition and set of ideas and practices that had defined my life. I separated myself from the language and the circles and the people who represented that world, and I couldn't wait to find that other thing, that better thing. And as I traveled and pushed and explored, I started realizing with a cringe that the road was leading me dangerously close to the start, and I was finding myself drawn against all odds, against my intentions, to this way of living, this way of Jesus, this way of passion and compassion that I had grown up in.

My parents, I think, were as surprised as I was. They watched me fall in love with several of the loveliest but most unsuitable boyfriends, watched me barrel down several of the most ridiculous paths, watched me learn from the same mistakes over and over and over until it seemed like maybe I wasn't learning at all.

There's a lot of pressure on pastors to coerce their kids into looking the part, or to distance themselves from kids whose mistakes reflect poorly on their churches. My parents did just the opposite: they flew across the country several times a year to be with me, to demonstrate to me that no matter how ferociously I fought for space in a world that felt like it had no room for me, they would be right there, right next to me, helping me fight and helping me make peace.

I loved those years. Those years made me believe in the journey and respect it, the way you respect deep water if you've ever swam out too far and been surprised by the waves. I know what that journey can do in people. I know what it did in me, and I don't take it lightly. I have some very sobering scars and memories that I carry

with me as reminders of that season. They remind me how dangerous that path is, and how beautiful.

Along the way, I've collected more questions than answers, but
I've fought for a few ideas that have formed a bed I can rest on, a life
I can make peace with, a dream I can cling to. I'm not a doctrinar-
ian, mostly because for me, doctrine is not the thing that God has
used to change my life. I'm a reader and a storyteller, and God chose
literature and story and poetry as the languages of my spiritual text.
To me, the Bible is a manifesto, a guide, a love letter, a story. To me,
life with God is prismatic, shocking, demanding, freeing. It's the
deepest stream, the blood in my veins, the stories and words of my
dreams and my middle-of-the-night prayers. I am still surprised on a
regular basis at the love I feel for the spirit of God, the deep respect
and emotion that I experience when I see an expanse of water or a
new baby or the kindness of strangers.

I'm immeasurably thankful to have been born into a community of faith. And I'm even more thankful that my community of
faith allowed me the space and freedom to travel my own distances
around and through the questions I needed to answer. I'm thankful for the patience and grace I was given, for the forgiveness I was
extended, and the guidance I needed.

I'm thankful for God's constant flickering and sparking flame
inside me, planted in me years ago and fighting to keep burning.
For a season, I didn't think it mattered much, but now I know that
tiny flame is the most precious thing I have, and that it can ignite a
forest fire inside any heart and can burn away a lifetime of apathy
and regret and distance.

22

Seamless

by Jessie van Eerden

Natalie and I found a broken crayfish in the stream below my house. The back of its shell was cracked, and some bloody pus was leaking out. We stared at the crayfish for a long time, eyes welling up with tears, certain in our hearts that its pain was intense.

Natalie was from town. Her mom had bought us cream-filled powdered donuts on the morning after her slumber party that May. She had, I think, packed different clothes when she had come to my house, the kind her mother would call "play clothes," not her usual bright name brands. I vaguely wondered if the creek water that seeped into her shoes troubled her as we gazed in solemnity and horror. We knew what we had to do.

I scoped out the creek bed and found a good-sized rock, one that required both of us to lift it. The whimpers started before we even dropped the stone, before the muted crunching sound or the ooze of brown blood. Then we just started wailing and running for home, never checking under the rock to see if the wounded creature was indeed put to rest or if its mangled body was still squirming. We held each other and sobbed in the tree house. Two tiny women with no desire at all to make heavy decisions for life or for death. But we had met a broken thing and thought it could never rightly live if it could not live whole.

Natalie and I grew apart in junior high and high school, moved on to different crowds and styles of clothes, and we forgot our murder of mercy at the creek. We did, however, come upon more fragmentation, broken backs, and bleeders. We ourselves would bleed once a month as well. We experienced the splitting off of selves inside of us, the adolescent us, and struggled awkwardly to choose the one that was good and right.

We haven't spoken in years, but I'm pretty sure that Natalie, like me, occasionally receives the gift of seeing people, just for a moment, as broken dolls. We get that glimpse of damaged parts. The men in the bus stop limp from some unknown wound; the women bend over strollers or carts and don't fully straighten, their skirt hems absently tucked into a high stocking. The huge rocks we could drop are nowhere to be found. We are bleeders all.

• • •

Sarah Liv and I are in the car, driving back to Washington, DC from a New York folk festival in late July. We left in the middle of Ani DiFranco's set: just Ani and an acoustic. We hated to leave, but we have to go in early tomorrow to the adult literacy agency where we work as stipend volunteers. We turn down my Gillian Welch tape and we start talking about a line from one of Ani's songs: *Move over, Mr. Holiness, and let the little people through.* We talk about how we are each deciding to handle the sacred vocabulary; she, with her Lutheran roots, and me, with my ingrained Bible-belt Methodism. We wonder if the words of our childhood faith-lives—words like *worship, praise, holiness*—have any real clout for us when we really stare them in the face as adults and when, out of the corner of our eyes, we see more and more brokenness in the world, in the city where we live, and in the basic reading classrooms where we teach grown men who puzzle over phonics and who may or may not have homes. Can we sing these worship-words, or recite them meaningfully as we walk past bus stops or begin a lesson on simple subjects and predicates? Don't words decompose anyway, like a dead pigeon in the alley? We should know by now to be paranoid around words that only attach and detach from meaning like chips of magnetic poetry on the fridge.

In the car tonight, the word *holiness* seems so demanding: some hand coming to stroke us, expecting bright pearl. It seems narrow and unforgiving, even unforgivable, like a father who uses a belt when the crime doesn't warrant it, and the child is left to make sense of the blue-black on her legs. Only, we're not the child—we've grown up in okay homes of church-going parents—but we're standing in the next room, the little people listening in on the hurt, standing empty and praiseless, at a loss for words.

Sarah Liv and I fall quiet and listen to Gillian's "Annabelle." We talk intermittently; we mention our heads of hair. She donated hers to kids with cancer when she got it cut. It meant a free haircut and someone's gorgeous auburn wig, but she cried the whole day for the loss. We consider stopping for a bite to eat: fast food at the next exit off the turnpike.

What's the point of exhausting already winded words? I grew up singing sacred words in my youth choir at Beatty Church in rural West Virginia, songs about the blessed poor in spirit, the morning's new mercies, the everlasting arms you could lean on. And we went into the Sunday school rooms for lessons on a holy Jesus, white and pasty on a flannel board, with ruddy disciples stuck up on the board beside him. It was a church like so many small churches, dotting the hillsides in small towns and dying out, like the towns' local hardware stores do when Wal-Marts move in. As a church kid, I spoke and sung the words with fervor, but now, since I've left home, the words at Beatty can seem deflated, part of an insular, insignificant community. Since I've left, I've sensed the loss: the sacred language goes limp in a world estranged from itself, a world that doesn't always consider the everlasting arms substantial enough to lean into. The loss I feel in the power of these words may be a kind of nostalgia, but for many of us who grew up in the church, I think it's more than that.

What's the point of exhausting these words—unless there is something to them that is still powerful? Something that could terrify or exhilarate beyond tired themes. Should we not try to claim the word bank of holies as our own? In the car, Sarah Liv and I wonder if, with a little sanding and polishing, they could be functional and relevant. Maybe. Or maybe we should just get new ones, but I'm not sure that we can.

• • •

For me, *holy* has to be more light than dark. Maybe it is whole. One big newness, unbroken, or if broken, then healed, or if not healed, then healing. To come into my own vocabulary means inspecting its foundation—built of an upbringing of supper talk and Beatty's revival services and nights of blubbering prayer on a blue gingham bedspread—and reconstructing the terms for myself. As I build it back, I know I will find a stubborn part, and I will have to struggle to go against the grain. It will seem easier and truer, though resigning, to make the saw sing and go the way of the old hardwood grain. It's difficult to make music any other way—to make something that matters and holds. Maybe I shouldn't try. Maybe nothing whole will emerge for me until I do try.

Sometimes there comes a moment when the sacred words still make music for me. With one voice, like a group of altos at the cathedral, they make sense—not because they're perfect, imposing words, but because they are my formative words: they gave me my first context for making meaning, for connecting with something larger than myself. They need, I'm convinced, constant re-imagining, as they shoot up like sprouts, in a memory or on a street corner, and I sit with them, bug-eyed, as I'd like to sit once again with a tiny bleeding crustacean. Very still, attentive. My reaction is visceral in these moments and my impulse both creative and completely undone. Re-imagined, worship-words take on body, become substance, beyond the liturgical phrase, and I can watch them come together, the way fragmented pieces create one huge mosaic on the side of a busted-up building.

• • •

Once, I inherited a dress, a hand-me-down from my sister. It was probably a gift to her from an Ohio relative, since it was store-bought and heavy knit material. I remember loving it up, thinking myself lucky to be small enough for the fit. The skirt part was bright yellow with red polka dots; it had a low, irregular seam where it connected to the bodice just past my hips and little-girl pad of belly. Smaller versions of the skirt flared in cuffs at the wrist. The bodice was all white except for a picture of a cat, not embroidered but attached like a decal, with a yellow and red ribbon tagging its ear. The dress was long-sleeved, a winter dress despite being knee-length. On the clothesline, its skirt would flutter like a freckled yellow poppy.

I remember the day I saw the dress on her.

I knew it was the same dress because it wasn't from a local store where just anybody could have gotten it, since it had been a gift from an Ohio relative, since it was knit, thick, warm.

I'd grown out of it finally, and, since I had no smaller siblings, Mom had packed it with the other worn-out clothes into a garbage bag for the county clothing center, for the last day of the month when they handed out clothes to the needy. And here was the girl who'd picked my dress from the lot. The yellow skirt fanned slightly as she spun around to speak to the girl behind her in line. The seam between skirt and bodice underlined her belly as it had mine. Our lines were passing as her class headed to recess and mine, an older class, to the cafeteria. Girls and boys swung on the railings around us.

I felt instantly charitable and instantly violated. The dress had obviously been handled, had gone through the wash a few times. One cuff had been sewn back on, its new thread conspicuous. I don't remember the girl's face, whether I found her pretty or coarse or dirty, but I clearly remember the weary dress and my restrained hand that could almost touch it.

I'd received so many used-up things: chairs, snowsuits, tops and bottoms, bikes, balls, shoes. But rarely had I given or tossed off, shed something that another person found valuable. I felt like the upper crust, begged from like a kid on McDonald Street, one of the doctors' kids. This girl was my beneficiary, and I was to be thanked.

But I only wanted my dress back. I wanted to be small, with a belly not so noticeable and with narrower shoulders that didn't strain the stitches. She had somehow crawled inside me, the used me, and sought promise and newness from a dress hopelessly faded: the red gone to a dull pink, the yellow pale, the cat face peeling at one ear, offering nothing. A pity flooded me. I knew that eye of longing all too well. Soon it would be an eye darkened and dulled by the dress's loose seams, by a flash of cold comparison as another body in a new jean skirt would swoop down on the bench beside this used yellow.

The girl and I passed and said nothing. Both our hair ribbons blew and trailed down our backs.

The girl and I did not know what we would do as women when people would beg from us, when we would wear our one dress to church and the same one to weddings and to luncheons, with a different necklace each time to make it seem new. As grownups, we would doubt our tricks would work and fear a blown cover. We would act as if it were a choice of deliberate prudence and simple living. We did not know if we would be the beggars.

The dress has to be an image of something holy, as though holiness were defined by longing itself. The single sight of a girl in a dress. She deals with the plain truth that shabby always shows. She seeks promise, honey, milk, star all her life.

Holy is single: one dress, worn old. Hold it, fold it, and smell the folds.

• • •

Once, when I was home on a visit from DC, Mom sewed my red bridesmaid dress for a wedding in late fall. She said to me, "Now, Jessie, it will look homemade," with a face tinged with worry over the thought of mismatched straps or fraying hems. She had sewn the bodice, and I tried it on like a halter top with my running shorts. I thought it looked sheen and satiny and clean in the wardrobe mirror. What does it mean to look homemade? "Why shouldn't it?" I asked her. Why make it *look* store-bought, as smooth as manufactured candy?

She tacked the bodice ribbon down late at night, in an effort to make sure it would match the other bridesmaids' for the pictures. The ribbon peeked out of the bodice like a bloom. In the middle of canning season, in between doctor visits with my grandparents, therapy appointments with Aunt Becky, in between caring for broken bodies, Mom fussed with this ribbon. She put love into a dress.

Holy emerges, sewn and mended. It's a tacked down ribbon.

Holy, you look homemade, you look stitched.

Why don't you want to bear your stitches and let them bloom into a new kind of right?

It is no wonder we are rendered wordless, with our eyes of longing unblinking before the world. We want to be seamless sheets, bright and holy in moonlight. We are looking to be consecrated, smoothed.

• • •

Four living creatures in John's Revelation are full of wings and eyes, sit before God, and say without ceasing: *Holy. Holy, holy, holy, the Lord God the Almighty, who was and is and is to come.* I want to be them for a moment, with my eyes full of perfection, my voice having to utter only a single word. Is it a smothering word? Is it my word? Maybe it's a word that drowns out the asking, which is also ready on the tip of my tongue.

• • •

Prophets of the old covenant spoke in oracles. They start off with something like: *The oracle that the prophet Habakkuk saw.* Then they go on to tell their ominous news of destruction and desolation. Sometimes they foresee a rebuilding, stone upon stone, a people's homeland fixed up. Sometimes they just ask. Isaiah, the prophet who in his oracle's fifty-seventh chapter said that God's name is Holy, collapsed from seeing God's glory and declared himself undone. Undone means not whole yet, like a quilt in a plastic bag, just pieced. Undone means not purified yet, with unclean lips that utter humanity's dirty words. Holy touched a hot coal to Isaiah's drawn mouth and gave him new words to say.

I would rather not be a prophet. I would rather be one who has eyes to see and ears to hear. One who fixes for a moment on something shimmery in what a prophet shares, then goes back and replays that vision over and over, selecting my own glowing visions as though they were a handful of moving marbles, cat's-eyes, the first revealings. I'd go on my back steps, holding these glimpses close as kittens and stroking them, sustaining them, alone.

I am one of the little people, wanting to know, despite myself, awaiting an oracle. I think I hold fast to you, Holy, as a child holds the string of a helium balloon: wrapped around twice, so I don't lose you. Mystified by all that fills you up so full. I don't have the words for it.

• • •

I am as empty and full as a glass of water on a cleared desk. I want a cup not so full with the booming of my own life. I want it to be full of hush to sip from. Maybe that's what holiness is, that hush, when all of our sacred words have been said and the silence follows. Sarah Liv can sense it better than I can, in the car as it nears midnight and she's the only one driving because I can't drive stick. We're tired and silent, sitting with the tensions in our own conversation about language, but feeling a life there, where we sit in our two bucket seats, a life pulsing beyond our own.

• • •

When I can be still, I stop trying to sound out holiness in words altogether, and I try only to picture it, looming there, among the words that are really only attempts. There was a boy, C. P., in my youth choir back at Beatty. He died as a teenager in a car wreck, but I remember that his face shone when he was a boy. Right now, I conjure him up, sitting in the pew with his folks—seeing what he sees.

C. P. pictures holiness in a squat:

And let us pray as our Lord taught us to pray: *Our Father who art in heaven, hallowed be Thy name. Hall-oh-wood.* Hallowed is holy, hallowed like hollowed, a hollowed out bowl on top of the altar. The prayers churn out one big voice from their throats—a droning with a pause sometimes after a word like *kingdom* or with hiss echoes after *trespasses.* A Big Voice, a small hand, C. P. covering his mouth as he yawns. His mouth widens, swallows some of the words.

Beside him, before prayer, his mom and dad shared a hymnbook in their hands. Now, the man's big hand keeps a finger marking the hymnal page; his other's in his pocket. Her hands hold each other closed. C. P. doesn't put his hands at all, except to his mouth as he yawns. The older congregants in the church laid hands on all three of them once for prayer, hands like leaves fallen just short of the ground, catching on a sleeve or shoulder.

To C. P., the hollow bowl is a beggar's bowl, empty, no beggar seen at the altar at all. If there were one, he'd have skin leathered by the sun and hands always open. The young C. P. yawns again, his mouth a new bowl, and his and hers, the man's and woman's are bowls, as the last beads of the string of all that fits in the bowl, before the *Amen*, rumbles on in the Big Voice:

For Thine is the kingdom

(pause)

C.P. crouches down, as if to shoot marbles.

The power

He pictures how a beggar would hold the bowl, between his squatting legs, want marking up his face like face paint.

And the glory forever.

Hallowed's bowl fits the boy's hands. It is not as heavy as he thought. He decides to want.

Amen.

• • •

Maybe holiness is a posture. The stooping and the asking.

There is room in holy for ask.

• • •

I know this guy, Richard, who pictures holiness in a bust:

A friend of a friend of my sister, Richard has quit his job to take a ten-year portrait-painting class. You could raise a family for ten years, trace a wife's face and neck and collect her quirks for a deep ten years. But he will study seeing and knowing for ten years. He will paint one bust for a year, over and over. He will know its chin line and every socket and curve in this full year of replication. He'll be drunk with the study of the single. The next year: a still life. One solid thing a year for ten years till the seeing drives him mad and he's a master and he sees the same face in a thousand shattered mirrors, pictures himself multiple and alone. But the jaw line, the jaw line is perfect.

I squint like Richard to focus in on holy. I stare till I see double, then triple, then many. I strive to master it, and the more I strive, the more it confounds me. Holy refuses to be mastered; it is only laid out like a scant trail of bread crumbs to lead me back from a cold bank of snow and a shivering perfect, to be grounded in a warm room with people of flesh and of love. A touch to a drawn face. A kiss that blooms.

• • •

I picture holiness as a roughed-up bleeding crayfish, twitching its pincher as it sits there by my friend Natalie's bright shoes. A broken, partial thing. A part of the mutilated world, with its rush of fears, its rush of hallelujahs.

• • •

Holy, at its root, means set apart. Bud Angus evangelized at Beatty one night and preached *entire sanctification in Christ*, separateness from the world, achievable perfection with the right faith and language and jaw line. But, imagine: perfect holiness. There are days when I think that all things shabby and split at the seams are holy, set apart to be loved utterly. To be won over in an intimate heap of promise. I want to be sanctified there.

• • •

The steps to my house are broken. We are two strips stitched together, Sarah Liv and I, we are two women in the space in a car, two friends having to prove *I've mastered, I'm different and grown, I have my own words for things now,* until we settle into one another and become two at one table at a fast food place, off the turnpike, our voices fluid and wavery and fast. And then still. Sarah Liv, you take one frail word and

I'll take another, and we will string them as we could popcorn and cranberries for a Christmas tree. I will beg from you. You will take parts of me and piece me together, meet me, the used me, on broken steps on a city street.

Hold my face as if it were a single stone.

About the Contributors

Jessica Belt writes about religion, growing up in Texas, and the eccentricities of urban living. Her nonfiction has appeared most recently in *Relief*. Jessica received her MFA from Lesley University, in Cambridge, Massachusetts, where she currently lives.

Paula Carter recently received her MFA in creative writing from Indiana University and is currently working as a freelance writer and editor in Columbus, Ohio. Her work has appeared in *Quick Fiction* and *Rhino*.

Kirsten Cruzen, after a lifetime of moving, married a native New Yorker and settled in New York City. She began her city experience teaching in a high-needs middle school with the New York Teaching Fellows Program.

Anne Dayton is the coauthor of several novels, including *Emily Ever After*, *The Book of Jane*, *The Miracle Girls*, and *Breaking Up Is Hard To Do*. She works in book publishing and lives in Brooklyn.

Andrea Palpant Dilley is a freelance writer and documentary producer based in Austin, Texas. Her writing has appeared in *Rock & Sling*, *The Global Citizen*, *Whitworth Today*, *Blood Orange Review*, *The Inlander*, and *The Spokesman-Review*. Her documentary work includes a series of human-interest vignettes broadcast nationally on the Hallmark Channel, a program entitled *Sudan: The Path to Peace*, which premiered at the Amnesty International Film Festival in Victoria, British Columbia, and a program entitled *In Time of War*, broadcast nationally on American Public Television.

Kimberly B. George graduated in 2003 from Westmont College with an English degree. She is passionate about interdisciplinary study and uses her creative writing to wrestle with the intersection of narrative, theology, psychology, and gender studies. Her essays and short stories have appeared in several print and online magazines including *Christian Feminism Today*, *Relief*, and BurnsideWritersCollective.com. She also co-writes a regular column with Letha Dawson Scanzoni titled 72–27: A Cross-Generational

Dialogue between Two Christian Feminists (http://eewc.com/72–27/) and keeps her own blog at faithandgender.blogspot.com.

Carla-Elaine Johnson completed her MFA in creative nonfiction at the University of Minnesota in 2007. She currently is at work on a memoir about her spiritual life entitled *Third Time Lucky: A Latebloomer's Spiritual Memoir*. Her work has appeared in *Dislocate*. She teaches in Minneapolis and lives in St. Paul, Minnesota.

Megan Kirschner (a pseudonym) recently left the publishing world to complete her degree in English. She has had pieces published with *The Kenyon Review*, *Broadside*, and *Red Cents*. She is the office and internet manager for a company that works with Web site and graphic design. She lives with her husband and son in Indiana.

Anastasia McAteer holds a master of divinity with a concentration in worship, theology, and the arts from Fuller Theological Seminary. Her interests include liturgical theology and the spirituality of food. Her blog, *Feminary*, has a worldwide readership of seminary students, clergy, and laypeople from many faith traditions. She has published reviews and essays online at *Christianity Today Movies*, *Downtown LA Life*, and *Art Source Los Angeles*. She lives in California with her husband John, a philosopher, and daughter Maggie. She remains a devoted Episcopalian.

Melanie Springer Mock is an associate professor in the Department of Writing and Literature at George Fox University in Newberg, Oregon. Her book *Writing Peace: The Unheard Voices of Mennonite Great War Objectors* was published by Cascadia in 2003, and her work has appeared in *Adoptive Families*, *Literary Mama*, *The Chronicle of Higher Education*, and *Brain, Child*, among other places. She is the mother of two seven-year-old sons.

Audrey Molina has a masters in Christian studies from Regent College in Vancouver, British Columbia. She has worked at the *Washington Post* and lives in the San Francisco Bay area.

Victoria Moon is a writer and mother currently residing in Marietta, Georgia. She has spent most of her writing life as a freelance journalist focusing on religious issues and popular culture for various regional and national publications. A 2004 graduate of Spalding University's MFA in writing program, her creative essays have appeared in *The Louisville Review*, *Relevant*, and *A Cup of Comfort* (Adams Media, 2002).

Shauna Niequist lives in the Chicago area with her husband Aaron, who is a worship leader, and their son Henry. She grew up at Willow Creek, then studied English and French literature at Westmont College, in Santa Barbara. She worked in student ministry at Willow Creek for five years and as the creative director at Mars Hill in Grand Rapids for three years.

Shauna's first book, *Cold Tangerines*, is a collection of essays about the extraordinary moments in our everyday lives. Her very favorite things are throwing dinner parties, taking full advantage of summers on the lake, and reading great books.

Hannah Faith Notess is the creative writing editor of *The Other Journal*. She earned an MFA in creative writing at Indiana University and was the 2008–2009 Milton Center Fellow in Creative Writing at *Image* journal and Seattle Pacific University. Her work has recently appeared in *Slate*, *The Christian Century*, *Mid-American Review*, and *Crab Orchard Review*, among other journals. She lives in Seattle.

Angie Romines is pursuing her MFA in creative writing at Ohio State University, and is getting used to a student body of more than sixty thousand after attending Christian schools for the past seventeen years.

Andrea Saylor grew up in Pennsylvania and studied English at Messiah College. She lives in Philadelphia, where she is pursuing a degree in international peace and conflict resolution.

Nicole Sheets' essays and book reviews have appeared in *Western Humanities Review*, *Quarterly West*, *North Dakota Quarterly*, and *Pilgrimage*. She has also published articles in several magazines and newspapers in her home state of West Virginia. Nicole is working on a nonfiction collection about her Peace Corps experience in the Republic of Moldova. She is a PhD candidate at the University of Utah and lives in Salt Lake City, Utah.

Shari MacDonald Strong (www.sharimacdonaldstrong.com) is the editor of *The Maternal Is Political: Women Writers at the Intersection of Motherhood and Social Change*. She has written about politics, spirituality, and motherhood at *Literary Mama* (www.literarymama.com), where she also serves as a senior editor. Her essay "On Wanting a Girl" appeared in the Seal Press anthology *It's a Girl: Women Writers on Raising Daughters* (edited by Andrea J. Buchanan), and her writing has appeared in a number of publications, including *Parents*, *Mamazine*, and *Geez* magazines. Shari worked as a writer, editor, and copywriter in the Christian publishing industry for fifteen years, most recently as a freelance contractor for a division of Random House, and she authored seven Christian romance novels for that market, as Shari MacDonald: *Sierra*, *Forget-Me-Not*, *Diamonds*, *Stardust*, *Love on the Run*, *A Match Made in Heaven*, and *The Perfect Wife*. She lives with her three children and photojournalist husband in Portland, Oregon.

Stephanie Tombari is a freelance writer whose work has appeared in *Geez*, *The Banner*, *Beyond Ordinary Living*, and *Faith Today*. She is also senior writer for the Christian Reformed World Relief Committee (CRWRC), a North American-based relief and development organization working in thirty countries around the world. Stephanie has traveled to Asia, Africa,

South America, and Europe to gather and retell stories of the poor, mistreated, and HIV-infected to North Americans.

Heather Baker Utley is the communications director for Youth Dynamics, a parachurch youth organization that ministers to teenagers across the Pacific Northwest. She grew up in the shadow of steel mills in a small town in Southeast Ohio. Prior to calling Washington state home, she acquired a BA in literature and international studies from Taylor University in Upland, Indiana, and spent five months in Kenya.

Jessie van Eerden holds an MFA in nonfiction from the University of Iowa. Her work has appeared in *Best American Spiritual Writing*, *Image*, *Geez*, *Oxford American*, *Riverteeth*, and other publications. She teaches at the Oregon Extension of Eastern University and lives in Ashland, Oregon, with her husband Mike.

Sara Zarr is the author of two critically acclaimed novels for young adults, *Story of a Girl* (a 2007 National Book Award finalist) and *Sweethearts*, both published by Little, Brown. She has also contributed to the anthologies *Does This Book Make Me Look Fat?: Stories about Loving—and Loathing—Your Body* (Clarion Books) and *Geektastic: Stories from the Nerd Herd* (Little, Brown). Her third novel, *Once Was Lost*, will be published in fall 2009. She lives in Salt Lake City, Utah, and online at sarazarr.com.